WILD
YOUR GARDEN

WILD
YOUR GARDEN

Create a sanctuary for nature

THE BUTTERFLY BROTHERS

CONTENTS

FOREWORD

We grew up in the nineties, completely immersed in the natural world. We spent our first years of childhood growing up in a wonderful, semi-detached Victorian house on a busy street in a small town. Looking out of the front bay window, we could see an average-sized gravel driveway, then the pavement and then the road. A large privet hedge housed the resident dunnocks, along with a mock orange, forsythia, and a flowering currant bush.

The back garden told a different story. The plot was relatively narrow but very, very long. We used to walk out into the garden, up the paved path along the edge of the lawn, past an old apple tree (Dad built us a fantastic treehouse there), and on to the bottom of the garden. There stood a big old shed that was completely engulfed by a huge climbing rose, while the area beside it contained a fantastic mixture of brambles, nettles, old sheets of plywood to pinch for den-building, and a compost bin full of creepy crawlies – including the largest house spider imaginable!

The front privet hedge wrapped around the side of the house and ran the full length of one side of the plot, providing a welcome retreat for the colony of house sparrows that lived there, a plentiful species back then. We would make occasional gaps in the hedge in order to carry out regular apple scrumping raids into neighbouring gardens at the end of summer.

On the opposite side of the garden was Mum's pride and joy – a wonderful border that she grew all sorts of great plants in. There, depending on the season, we'd enjoy irises, geraniums, snowdrops, sunflowers, gooseberry bushes, violets, and bluebells. Mum's interest in gardening, combined with Dad's passion for fishing and a childhood spent searching for birds' nests, was bound to shape us into enthusiastic naturalists.

We would spend hours kneeling beside the wildlife pond in our back garden.

Later, we moved to the other side of town, into a small bungalow surrounded by conifers. One day, Dad proudly brought home the battered old shell of a fibreglass pond. As he placed it down on the ground, he miscalculated the position of one of the conifer stumps, which smashed straight through its middle! The shell was soon repaired, and after much digging the pond was finished. On the 4th August 1996, we officially sat beside our first ever wildlife pond. It's safe to say this was the most influential moment of our childhoods.

We spent countless hours knelt beside the water's edge, spotting water boatmen, turning over stones looking for frogs, and stealing old maggots from Dad's bait box and tying them to fishing line to catch greedy smooth newts from holes in the weed. We would often ask to stay up past our bedtime to watch bats hunting insects over the pond.

The "feral" childhood we had back then is now a very rare thing indeed. The ever-growing demand for new housing estates has resulted in a huge loss of wild places, such as derelict brownfield sites and waste ground, where children and wildlife could happily coexist.

By reimagining how we use our gardens, we can all do our bit
to support local wildlife and tackle the climate crisis.

And as for our own gardens, how many of us can honestly say we live in an
area rich in birdsong, hedgehogs, bats, and dragonflies? A peek into a
neighbour's garden may reveal nothing but mown grass and paving, or –
worse still – artificial grass and plastic plants. How many fences nowadays
have holes or gaps for hedgehogs to use as they roam the neighbourhood?
How many ponds are there in the other gardens on the street for the local
frogs and newts? How can birds and bats access roof spaces now that
builders use tightly fitting plastic soffits and fascia boards?

Even the green space we do have is often effectively sterile. Flower
beds and ornamental shrubs are more often than not tainted by slug
pellets and chemical insecticides. Then there's our choice of plants: exotics
may look stunning, but they don't support our invertebrate species nearly
as well as natives do.

We only need to think back to primary school lessons about the food chain to realize what a problem this is. Vegetation is eaten by insects, which in turn are preyed upon by birds, mammals, amphibians, reptiles, and so on. If the insects are dying off due to chemicals and non-native plants, what does that mean for the rest of our native wildlife?

Throughout the world, natural habitats are under threat. In Europe, for instance, more than 50 per cent of grasslands are endangered or vulnerable, while the UK is estimated to have lost more than 97 per cent of its meadows and at least a quarter of a million miles of hedgerow since WW2. Now, more than ever before, our wildlife is in trouble. Many species, from wildflowers to great crested newts, grasshoppers to house sparrows, are in desperate need of our help (and that's without even mentioning the climate crisis).

But, in spite of all the doom and gloom, there is hope – and it starts on our own doorsteps.

Imagine what would happen if we transformed our outdoor spaces – the rural gardens, the urban balconies, and everything in between – and turned them into spaces for nature; if everyone with the means to do so planted a tree, put up a bird box, dug a pond, and let the grass grow long; if we reclaimed the wilder, richer, more birdsong-filled gardens of our childhoods. All it would take is for a few people on each street to work together, and before long we would create a nationwide network of habitats. By taking positive steps in our own gardens, no matter how small, together we can really make a difference.

Joel Ashton

ASSESS YOUR SPACE

Take a moment to think about how you can maximize the wildlife potential of your garden – what you want to keep, what you want to add, and how you want to bring it all together.

INTRODUCTION

It's very easy to think of a wildlife garden as a mass of brambles, nettles, and a few trees and shrubs. This stereotype can put off many gardeners who would hate to see their beloved patch become an overgrown mess, while others might use it as an excuse to neglect their garden and let nature completely take over.

In many respects it's true that, if left to its own devices, nature will create a range of habitats that are finely balanced to provide all the food, shelter, and nesting sites for a wide range of creatures. But rewilding a garden – inviting nature back into a space that we have claimed for ourselves – requires some input on our part in order to create a space that will appeal to both humans and wildlife alike.

So, before you pick up a spade and start digging, take some time to reflect on what you want to achieve with your wildlife garden. Some of these considerations might be practical. How much do you want to spend? Where will you put the bins? Will your neighbour be happy if you decide to take out the fence?

A great wildlife garden is all about the preparation and planning. Hold off on the digging until you've worked out what you want where.

You also need to think about how best to support and encourage the wildlife you want to attract to your garden. Planning the best place to situate a pond could mean the difference between an empty, algae-filled pool of water and a thriving ecosystem teeming with life, while what you choose to do with your boundaries and paved surfaces will determine the number and variety of plant species you can introduce into the space. If anything, design is even more crucial in a wildlife garden than in a standard one, as you aren't just designing for yourself and your family: you're designing for nature.

If you're now asking yourself "where do I start?" and wondering how on earth you are going to wild your garden, don't worry. This chapter will take you through all the basics: how to work out your garden's aspect, make the most of existing features, and what to think about when considering new additions – be it a pond, a path, a nectar border, or a meadow. We'll even show you a simple plan of a newly rewilded garden, so you can see just how much you can achieve, no matter how much outdoor space you have.

KNOW YOUR GARDEN'S ASPECT

Before you embark on a big project, take some time to work out your garden's aspect.

"Aspect" – which direction an outdoor space faces – is crucial when planning any new garden design. Whether a garden faces north, south, east, or west will determine which areas receive full sun, partial sun, partial shade, or full shade as the sun moves through the sky. This, in turn, influences which plant species or habitat types will do best in a particular area, and what wildlife will visit.

To discover the aspect of a garden (or any other form of outdoor space, such as a balcony), grab a compass or use an app on your phone and stand against the wall of the house (at the back or the front) or the balcony door. The direction your compass points is your garden's aspect.

Knowing your garden's aspect will help when it comes to planning out the placement of any new features, but it's also a good idea to observe how the levels of shade cast across your outdoor space change with the seasons before making any key decisions, as this will also influence considerations such as where to plant those new silver birch trees or where best to site a new pond.

One thing to remember with wildlife gardening is that sun isn't everything. Don't be put off by the idea of shady areas: while some species will enjoy basking in the sun, others will love a shady patch. Whatever your garden's aspect, there will be plenty of plants suited to it (see pages 182–86); you just need to know what will work.

A NORTH-FACING GARDEN

If your garden faces north, you wouldn't want to plant tall or medium-sized trees near your house, as they may end up casting shade over the centre of the garden. Instead, position them nearer the bottom of the garden; this will ensure that any central garden features stay in the sun for most of the day. After all, insects are heat-loving creatures, so will appreciate being warmed by the sun while they sup nectar from a flower.

AN EAST-FACING GARDEN

Watching the sun rise, with the sunlight streaming through the windows first thing in the morning, is a great way to start the day if you have an east-facing garden. It does, however, mean that the garden is likely to be in relative shade in the afternoon. If you locate new nectar borders too close to the house, for instance, insects will visit the border in the morning sun, but may nip over the fence in the afternoon to enjoy a neighbour's sunny spots.

A WEST-FACING GARDEN

If your garden faces west, it will start the day in shade before becoming warm and sunny in the afternoon. Plant your nectar border or cornfield meadow away from the house to avoid casting morning shade and maximize available sun for the small creatures, such as hoverflies, damselflies, and newts, who rely on the sun to warm up and get going. Likewise, aquatic invertebrates and amphibians also love to bask in the shallow, sun-drenched margins of a pond first thing in the morning, so position any water features away from this early shade.

A SOUTH-FACING GARDEN

On average, south-facing gardens receive the most sunshine throughout the day. This is great for most wildlife, but it does mean you'll also have to think about creating some shady refuge – for wildlife and people alike. Positioning trees towards the bottom of a plot, for example, affords some welcome shade from the midday sun, but such shade will have petered out before it reaches the middle of the garden, leaving a nice sunny spot for a pond. Planting a flowering lawn or wildflower meadow in an area that's always sunny allows the nectar-loving insects a much longer feeding time – we've seen butterflies in July feeding until 8pm in the last splashes of sunshine in the corner of a south-facing garden.

WORK WITH EXISTING FEATURES

It's very easy to want to put your stamp on a newly inherited garden, but please don't follow the "let's rip it out and start again" philosophy. Before you completely overhaul the planting within the space, take a moment to consider the benefits of keeping at least some of the established vegetation. You never know – that climber on your fence that you're thinking of getting rid of may just be the only safe refuge for birds in your garden. Without such cover, birds will desert the plot since they won't have anywhere to hide from predators, whether that be a sparrowhawk or the neighbour's cat.

EMBRACE MATURE PLANTS

A garden with mature trees, shrubs, and climbers is a bonus to wildlife. While some of these may not be in exactly the right place for your new garden scheme, we urge you to settle on a design that includes them, because even a single mature tree is an invaluable asset to both local wildlife and the ongoing fight against climate change. We've all heard the message that we need to be planting more trees to combat the climate crisis, because they take carbon dioxide out of the atmosphere as they grow. However, this good work should never be done at the expense of removing what trees we already have. Mature trees hold on to the carbon that they took in while they grew; if they are chopped down, they then release that carbon back into the atmosphere.

It's also easy to dismiss non-native trees and shrubs. Natives like silver birch, holly, rowan, oak, and ash are all excellent choices when planting new trees, but they should not be planted instead of an established tree with an established ecosystem simply because it isn't classed as a true native. Sycamore, for example, which was first introduced to the UK in the 1500s, supports countless aphids, which, in turn, provide valuable food for birds such as blue tits for feeding their young. Likewise, embrace established non-native shrubs when they are beneficial to local wildlife, such as mahonia and forsythia for their bright winter flowers and vital source of nectar for early emerging bees and other insects.

If you really aren't keen on the appearance of an established tree or shrub, there may well be an alternative to digging it up. For example, you could plant a dog rose at the base of a shrub; given time, it will grow through and ultimately cover the old plant. As a last resort, if you must cut a tree down, consider leaving the stump in place, as the standing deadwood will provide a vital (and rare) insect habitat (see also page 169).

Many of the wildlife gardens we're asked to design are in "new build" properties, almost all of which are bordered by new fences with no native hedges in sight. As you may guess, hedges trump fencing on the habitat front (see pages 32–39), so if you are lucky enough to acquire a new garden with an existing hedge, please consider keeping it as a boundary.

RETHINK THE LAWN

Many lawns may be undiscovered habitats in their own right. While mowing a lawn is akin to sheep grazing on grassland, just like that grassland, the lawn may already contain a fantastic array of wildflowers. We've seen many wild orchids, ox-eye daisies, or bird's-foot trefoil

"pop up" in a lawn once the mower has been relegated to the shed. So, boosting your garden's wildflower numbers could be as simple as letting the grass grow longer in spring – just imagine what wildflowers might emerge. Another option to boost an existing lawn's wildlife potential is to transform it into a flowering lawn (see pages 134–41); it's a relatively quick and satisfying project to take on.

A cluster of bird's-foot trefoil adds a great source of nectar in this flowering lawn.

PLAN FOR NEW FEATURES

Now that you've established which way the garden faces and what features you wish to retain, it's time to start the fun bit – what you want to add to the garden. If you can consider wildlife at every stage of planning your new features, it'll mean the difference between occasional visitors dropping in to feed before moving on and wildlife deciding to call your garden its new home. So, grab a pencil and let's get plotting!

BOUNDARIES

First, take a good look at the boundaries of the garden. Any dilapidated fences should be removed; this will provide you with an opportunity to install something a little more wildlife-friendly. Unless you or your

A native hedgerow (see pages 32–39) doubles up as both a boundary and a refuge for wildlife.

neighbour has a dog, a boundary doesn't have to be solid; a native hedgerow (see pages 32–39) is both cheaper and more attractive than a fence, plus the benefits of a hedge for wildlife are huge. If there's an existing fence to work with, transform it into something wilder with the addition of some trellis and some climbers (see pages 46–51); this design offers sanctuary and a source of food for birds and insects alike. Make sure to add a few hedgehog gaps, too (see page 48).

TREES AND SHRUBS

Next, consider the "backbone" of your wildlife garden – the trees and shrubs. Depending on your space's aspect (see pages 14–15), research which native trees and shrubs you'd like to include (see pages 182–86); be sure to make a note of how high they grow and how wide they spread as this may impact how far apart and where exactly you will plant them. The RHS website is also a good place to look for all such information.

This apple tree acts as an eye-catching focal point in the centre of the garden.

It's a good idea to keep trees and hedges to the perimeters of a garden (particularly in smaller gardens) to leave an opening in the middle for other features, similar to how a woodland edge would appear in the wild (see page 24). That being said, there is no harm in having a smaller "feature tree" – a rowan is ideal – nearer the house to entice birds to feed where you can watch them more easily.

WILDLIFE PONDS

Once you've plotted positions for the trees and shrubs, turn your attention next to the wildlife pond, which ideally needs a sunny spot; this

Site ponds at a comfortable distance away from
boundaries to make sure you can access them easily.

will encourage dragonflies to flock there throughout the summer. Position
any pond away from the reaches of large tree branches because excess
leaf litter in the autumn can turn the water black and add unwanted
nutritional value to the pondwater. It's also a good idea to locate the
pond away from any boundaries to prevent excessive shading from
fences or hedges in the morning or afternoon. Siting a pond near a
boundary can also make it difficult to access hedges or climbing plants
when the time comes to prune or cut them back. In essence, a pond slap
bang in the middle of the garden is ideal.

Many people feel a wildlife pond should merge into the background
and be tucked away in the corner of a garden, but if installed as a central
feature, even near the house, and planted correctly, it creates a stunning
water feature and attracts a huge and diverse range of wildlife.

BIODIVERSE SEATING AREAS

Patios are a main feature of many back gardens. It's useful to have a flat,
practical area of hard standing to sit and relax on, particularly when eating
and drinking in the warmer months. But rather than opt for the normal

paving slabs laid closely together with a small mortar joint between them, which can cause drainage issues (see page 23), why not consider something much more wildlife friendly here, too? For past patios, we've dug down deeply and then laid sandstone paving slabs with large joints between, which we've filled with soil and then added nectar-rich plants to the mix – great for pollinators and equally great for those sitting there, too.

When choosing plants for these types of spaces, look for tough species that can tolerate plenty of rough treatment from feet and chair legs. Thyme, bird's-foot trefoil, horseshoe vetch, kidney vetch, and rock rose work really well in such high-traffic areas. Herbs, such as wild marjoram, wild basil, and chives, work well towards the edges, as do lavender varieties and hyssop. These are purely suggestions; experiment with these spaces and you may well be surprised at what will self-seed and thrive between the paving slabs. One thing is certain, such patios will be full of colour, scent, and beautiful pollinating insects.

LINKING PATHS

Now that the plans for the main features of your garden are in place, you'll need to link them all together. There are two main considerations for this: where you place your paths and the material you use to create them.

First, consider which places you'll need to access regularly, such as a shed or compost heap, or garden features that you expect to visit often – your wildlife pond, for instance. These will be high-traffic pathways. Think about how you'll move around the garden to reach these areas: would you prefer a straight path from here to there, or one that takes a circuitous route around the garden? Once these practicalities are decided, move onto areas of lower traffic. For instance, you might want to take a stroll past the fringes of a fruit tree (with its tasty bounty at the right time of year), then stop at a bench near the pond for a little rest before crossing the flowering lawn to return to the back door.

Once you have an idea of the network of paths you want to create, it's time to think about the best materials for the job. We often use compacted gravel for high-traffic areas. This self-binding aggregate looks natural, creates soft edges, drains well, and avoids you having to set concrete slabs or bricks into the ground. It's also easy to walk on: you won't get muddy

Compacted gravel paths are a great option for routes
that will receive a lot of foot traffic.

feet during the autumn and winter months, and its compacted surface
means that it can support the weight of a heavy wheelbarrow. Wood chips,
bordered by natural logs or timber gravel boards, are another easy option
for pathways. Not only do such paths look natural – especially weaving
between trees and along native hedgerows – but the chippings also slowly
decay over time, providing an all-important deadwood habitat within the
garden (although it also means that the pathways will need to be topped
up now and then). Look for sustainably sourced wood chip from garden
centres, or talk to a local tree surgeon, who'll almost definitely be able to
supply you with the quantity you need for your paths.

Finally, for wild, grassy areas and those with the lowest amount of foot
traffic, you don't need to lay down any materials: simply mow a route

through the grass, avoiding any areas where you know that bulbs or clumps of flowers are likely to emerge. This works particularly well between spring and autumn, when we naturally spend more time in the garden and the ground is drier. Mowing pathways is also a good way of combatting particularly troublesome and vigorous vegetation; for example, mowing for a season over the top of emerging docks, thistles, and brambles will weaken them greatly and even make them disappear altogether.

PATIOS AND PARKING

We've left this one to last, as we prefer to avoid areas of hard paving wherever possible. Every year, there are fewer and fewer places where humans haven't put down hard, artificial surfaces. Paving is everywhere: it's in our towns and cities as tarmac roads, car parks, and pavements; around our homes, there are block-paved driveways and large patios. Every time rain falls, it lands on all these hard surfaces, running off quickly into our drainage systems, putting more and more pressure on them.

Try looking at paved areas in an altogether different way – one that considers water run-off and creates opportunities for growing wildflowers. If parking on a front drive is unavoidable, install a gravel driveway, as this would allow rainwater to soak through at a slow pace and create a perfect site for growing wildflowers. Kidney vetch, viper's bugloss, and wild strawberry love scrambling among gravel, while in nearby gravelly border edges, non-natives such as red valerian and verbena bonariensis will thrive. Planting in this way creates a delightful front garden while also providing pollinators with access to plenty of wildflowers.

If you need to pave over part of your plot, space the stones apart and plant low-growing species in the gaps.

PLANT FOR NATURE

By this stage, you should know your garden's aspect and have planned out where to site all the fixed features of your new garden, including trees and shrubs. Now, it's time to focus on the rest of your planting choices: those softer features that will really bring your new garden to life.

RECREATE A WOODLAND EDGE

A successful wild garden is one that takes its inspiration from natural habitats and offers a "home from home" for native wildlife. To achieve this, we recommend keeping in mind what we consider to be the optimum habitat found in the wild: the woodland edge. This mix of trees, shrubs, and wildflowers, combined with elements of sun and shade, provides a bounty of food and shelter for everything from badgers to blue tits and aphids to ants.

So, what does all this mean when it comes to garden design? In short, it's all about creating a sliding scale of height. Starting with those trees and larger shrubs around the perimeter of the garden (see pages 28–57), plot the positions of your remaining plants – your smaller shrubs, nectar borders, and so on – so that the smaller species will be located nearer to the centre of the garden. This approach will leave you with an opening, similar to a woodland clearing, where you can situate any ponds or wildflower meadows. Of course, you don't need to stick to this approach rigidly. For example, you might want to have a small "feature" tree, such as a rowan, in the middle of your meadow area to entice birds to feed nearer to the house where you can see them. Nevertheless, on the whole, we've found the woodland edge approach to be a useful starting point when planning wildlife gardens of all sizes and aspects, and recommend you give it a try.

NECTAR BORDERS

These flower-rich features (see pages 92–111) are integral to any well-designed wildlife garden. They are the link between formal and wild: key to creating that sense of formality that so many of us want from our gardens, while also being vital sources of nectar and breeding grounds for many different insect species – provided that they are planted in the right location. In simple terms, nectar borders are best positioned in sunny spots; whether that means morning or afternoon sun will depend on your aspect (see pages 14–15). A warmer location will encourage insects to buzz around and feed for longer, which in turn will attract birds and other larger species to your garden. Nectar-rich flowers also help to visually soften the bottom of fences and walls.

MEADOWS AND LAWNS

The beauty of a meadow is that it can take any shape, making it the ideal feature to plan last, once you know where all your other elements are going to go. They can be any size, too – we've transformed an area as small as 2sq m (22sq ft) into an amazing floral space. In addition to a meadow, a flowering lawn (see pages 134–41) mown on a high setting can provide the perfect transition between the formal edge of a patio and the more informal meadow area towards the centre or rear of a garden. You can even lay wildflower turf (available online) to achieve instant results, and treat it as a meadow or flowering lawn as the years go by – just be sure to buy a plastic-free variety.

VERTICAL SPACES

When planning a garden, it's quite easy to focus on the "flat" options, such as paving, lawn, pond, and paths. However, making use of vertical space, particularly in small outdoor areas and on balconies, can really boost the wildlife potential of your plot. For example, if your boundary incorporates a garage wall, try adding some horizontal wires to encourage and guide the growth of climbing plants, such as old man's beard or honeysuckle. Wooden archways or pergolas can perform the same role, while also doubling up as perfect spots for a butterfly chrysalis to hide away from predation – we've seen 15 or so chrysalises on the dry underside of a timber ledge of a pergola before.

These vertical spaces, once covered in climbing plants, can even make ideal habitats for resident house sparrows, and provide a great spot for siting a robin box (see pages 160–65).

PLAN YOUR GARDEN DESIGN

Once you have an idea of what you might like to include in your new wildlife garden, it's time to draw up a plan. Here, we have an example of a 10 x 15m (33 x 49ft) garden, featuring a large patio, a lawn, some mixed borders, and a few existing trees at the back (see right). Opposite, you can see how the garden could look – and just how many different habitats you can squeeze into a space of that size.

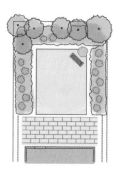

Before

1 Most of the existing trees and shrubs will be retained in order to maintain the habitat for birds and bats. To give the space a "woodland edge" feel, a variety of additional species will be planted alongside them.

2 To make the most of vertical space, a layer of trellis will be secured to the left- and right-hand boundary fences. With the addition of climbing plants, this "wild fence" will create ideal conditions for nesting birds (see pages 46–51).

3 This stretch of hedgerow along the right-hand fence will create a corridor for birds to move up and down the garden and access the feeder, which is positioned on the flowering lawn nearby.

4 Positioned in the centre of the garden, away from the trees and shrubs to avoid leaf litter and shade, this natural pond will be the focal point of the garden. Without a doubt, this will be the area that will support the most wildlife.

5 This T-shaped nectar border will be a colourful addition to the edge of the patio, where the garden's owners can comfortably sit and enjoy the visiting bees and butterflies. Its location also ensures that it will receive sun for as much of the day as possible.

6 By adapting a patch of the existing lawn, this flowering lawn will act as a great transition between the formal paving and the wildflower meadow beyond. This area (up to the dotted line) will be mown regularly on a high setting.

7 The meadow will be the garden's main attraction for insects in the summer months. Unlike the flowering lawn, the meadow will only be mown once a year, although you could always add one or two mown paths through the tall grasses if access is needed.

8 Placed at the edge of the woodland area, the bench will be the perfect place to sit and observe the flora and fauna of the garden. The trees will provide shade during the summer.

9 The compost bin (see pages 156–59) will need to sit somewhere where it can receive sun for a good portion of the day. The taller plants in the nectar border will help to discreetly hide the bin from the house.

10 A few log piles will be located in and around the woodland area to create additional habitat and hibernating potential, while others will be placed in a spot where they will receive morning sun, to encourage reptiles and amphibians to warm up on them.

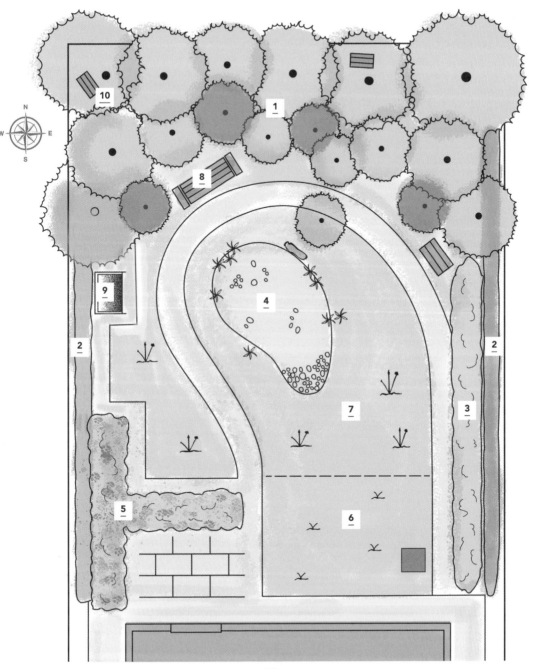

After

TREES
AND SHRUBS

Start thinking about trees and shrubs in
a whole new way: as biodiverse habitats,
as landmarks for flying wildlife, as a
natural form of flood defence, and
as invaluable carbon sinks.

INTRODUCTION

If we look at the natural world in ecological terms, it quickly becomes apparent just how rich the woodland edge can be. The area where a woodland meets another habitat – be it a grassy clearing, an area of heathland or downland with scattered scrub, or even a coastal dune system – is a uniquely biodiverse place, typically supporting a multitude of plant and animal species (even more so if a water source is also present).

So, how does this translate to the context of a residential garden? Well, first, gardens are a wonderful refuge, a real sanctuary in so many ways. Think of a bird flying over a suburban housing estate. The first place the bird looks for rest is in a decent-sized tree or, better still, a thick cluster of trees and shrubs of different heights and densities – a mini-copse, really.

Second, trees can be vital landmarks for flying visitors. Picture a bat emerging from its roost at dusk: it will rely on the presence of trees, hedges, and mini-copses for easy navigation while hunting for flying insects.

Third, trees and shrubs mean food to many species in a myriad of ways. Not only are the leaves of native trees and shrubs critical for so many invertebrates to feed on (whether in their adult or larval stage), but their

> Trees and shrubs are the
> essential "backbone" to any
> plot – you simply cannot
> have a good wildlife garden
> without them.

fruits and seeds can also sustain a range of different creatures throughout the year. Let's look at a rowan tree: many species of moth larvae, including grey dagger and brimstone, feed on its leaves in spring; bees and other pollinating insects enjoy the rich nectar of its plentiful flowers in summer; starlings and winter-visiting waxwings feast on its ripe berries; and even fallen and decaying branches are munched on by beetle larvae.

Finally, shrubs and particularly trees benefit us and our environments enormously. Not only do they capture carbon and produce oxygen, but trees can also slow down the effects of flooding by absorbing large volumes of water. In the summer, mature trees cool down their immediate surroundings by offering welcome shade, and come autumn their falling leaves act as a fantastic, nutrient-rich mulch to improve the underlying soil.

In this chapter we'll cover a range of creative ways you can incorporate trees and shrubs into your wildlife garden. Even if you think you don't have room to plant a tree or shrub, take a look at our list of suggested species (see pages 182–186) before ruling it out entirely. In our opinion, you simply cannot have a good wildlife garden without them.

Observe nature's changing
seasons through your
newly planted hedge and
reconnect with local wildlife.

A NATIVE HEDGEROW

Imagine a typical countryside scene. You will almost certainly see stretches of hedgerows growing along field boundaries, weaving their way across the landscape. These beautiful living tapestries are more than just a division between two parcels of land – they are a precious refuge for wildlife and a vital corridor between habitats.

If you are as passionate about wildlife as we are, you might have already noticed what an amazingly busy place a well-managed hedge can be. If you have an existing hedge, taking a more relaxed approach to how and when you cut it (see page 39) can reap huge benefits for its inhabitants, especially if you time it right: ideally, after the last of the winter berries have been produced, but before nesting season begins.

Or, better yet, if your garden's boundary is marked by an old fence or brick wall, why not read on and find out how you can replace the boundary with a native hedge of your own?

Let go of the idea that a hedge needs
to be box-shaped and trimmed twice a
year, and wildlife will thank you for it.

We give new hedges a hard prune to encourage dense growth, leaving just 15–20cm (6–8in) of stem behind. The image above was taken after we had completed cutting the hedge (along with other pruning work); you can just about see the remaining stems in the bed on the left.

To encourage the hedgerow to develop faster, keep the base free of weeds for the first two to three years, so that the hedges will not need to compete for nutrients. Within four to five years, the hedgerow will become fully established, providing shelter for nesting birds and other garden visitors.

WHAT TO PLANT

Most shrubs and trees are suitable for hedging, although larger tree species are best avoided in an average-sized garden. All the species on the Plant List (see pages 182–86) will grow well in sunshine; however, if your hedge is in a shady location consider choosing from holly, yew, box, dogwood, and hazel. We recommend choosing a few different species, in order to provide garden visitors with a variety of food sources throughout the year.

You can buy your plants either in containers or as bare-root specimens. Bare-root plants are much more cost-effective and, if properly looked after, they will establish just as quickly as container-grown versions. They are also easier and faster to plant when bare root, which is especially useful if you are planning a long hedge. Choose specimens around 60–90cm (24–36in) in size; any larger and they may be difficult to handle during planting.

It's always best to buy bare-root plants as near to your proposed planting date as possible. They will probably be supplied in a sack, so make sure that the roots are kept covered and stored somewhere cool and moist. Do not let them dry out. If you must buy them in advance, dig a hole somewhere in the garden and "plant" the whole bundle into the ground temporarily. This process – "heeling in"– is the best way of storing plants to keep them healthy until you need them.

PREPARING THE GROUND

The best time to plant a native hedge is between December and March. Find the line that marks the definite boundary and plan to position the hedge plants at least 30cm (12in) back from that. Otherwise, you may find you are constantly cutting them back too hard on the side they overhang a pavement or a neighbour's garden.

Once you have decided on the exact location and position of your new hedge, prepare the ground to give your plants the best possible start in life. Dig over a strip of

YOU COULD GROW...

ALDER

ALDER OR COMMON BUCKTHORN

CRAB APPLE

DOG ROSE

DOGWOOD

FIELD MAPLE

GOAT WILLOW

GUELDER ROSE

HAWTHORN

HAZEL

HOLLY

SPINDLE

WAYFARING TREE

WILD PRIVET

earth approximately 50cm (20in) wide, removing all stones and debris as well as any vegetation. This will give you good, workable soil – perfect for new roots to establish themselves easily. Finally, boost the soil's fertility and mix in some good organic matter, such as compost or leaf mould, into the soil. Homemade compost is ideal (see pages 156–59).

PLANTING THE HEDGE

Once the ground is thoroughly prepared, it is planting time. As a general rule of thumb, space your plants 25cm (10in) apart as a single continuous row, grouping each species in blocks of seven (for example, seven hawthorn, seven field maple, and so on). The plants will establish quickly and will fill out to form a dense, varied hedgerow. As you would for any tree or shrub, dig a hole for each plant that is large enough to accommodate its roots easily and make sure the bottom of the hole isn't compacted. Place the roots into the hole, keeping the line where the top of the roots start level with the ground – this is crucial for the plant to continue growing at the same level as it was previously. Backfill the hole with soil and firm around the roots with the heel of your boot. You don't necessarily have to water the plants once they are in the ground, unless it's very dry and mild. Finally, spread a 5cm (2in) layer of mulch (wood chippings or compost) over the soil.

Within a month or two, you'll need to give your new hedge a hard prune, by cutting each plant down until just 15–20cm (6–8in) of stem remains. This might sound extreme but, as with coppicing (see pages 40–45), the process encourages the young plants to grow more stems, which will help to achieve a denser and faster-growing hedgerow.

WHO LIVES THERE

Many species of birds use hedgerows to navigate the landscape, to roost and shelter in, and to feed from. During the breeding season, certain species including whitethroats, linnets, and yellowhammers almost entirely rely on hedgerows to build their nests in.

A Hawthorn (left) and guelder rose (right) **B** The fresh spring growth of a mixed hedge can teem with insect life. **C** To guarantee a constant supply of berries, cut back one half of the hedge one year and the other half the next.

YOU COULD HELP...

BLACKBIRD

DUNNOCK

HEDGEHOG

LINNET

ORANGE TIP BUTTERFLY

COMMON PIPISTRELLE

ROBIN

WHITETHROAT

WOOD MOUSE

YELLOWHAMMER

Bats use hedges as landmarks to navigate, feeding on the insects that rise from them at dusk. Wood mice and hedgehogs also forage through the bottom of the hedge, and many species of moth lay their eggs on the leaves of the diverse range of native species that a hedgerow can offer.

By sowing garlic mustard beneath your hedge, you can create the ideal habitat for the beautiful orange tip butterfly (see above). If you do sow garlic mustard, do not cut the hedge until April, after the butterflies emerge.

LOOKING AFTER THE HEDGE

With your hedge in place, sit back and wait for spring to work its magic. In April new growth will appear from the pruned stems. During the first year, while the plants are putting roots down, make sure to water the hedge well, and to pull out any weeds that might compete for nutrients in the soil.

1 Also known as "Jack-by-the-hedge", garlic mustard offers the ideal habitat for orange tip butterflies to lay their eggs. **2** The caterpillars have evolved to match the colour of the plant's seed pods. **3** The orange tip's unusually shaped chrysalis can be hard to spot. **4** The butterfly can be seen between April and June.

By the second year, the hedge will grow strongly, and some species (such as goat willow and dog rose) may be ready for their first cut. For others, you may not find that any cutting back is necessary until at least the third year of growth. In any case, keep any cutting to a minimum, and time the cut to suit the needs of the wildlife who live in, and feed on, the hedgerow. We find that March is usually best: this allows birds and other creatures to feed on the plants' berries throughout autumn and winter, but is early enough to avoid disturbing any nesting birds. One exception to this rule would be in cases where you've sown garlic mustard beneath the hedge, as a March cut may well disturb the orange tip butterfly's life cycle (see opposite).

A good long-term management plan would be to cut each side once every three years. For example, start with the top of the hedge the first year, then cut the side facing the garden the next year, and the last side the year after. Once the hedge is mature, this relaxed approach to trimming ensures there will always be berries and cover available every year.

Create a mosaic of habitats
that provide both shelter and
a plentiful source of food for
birds and other species.

A COPPICE BELT

When we think of wildlife in a garden, birds tend to be what spring to mind first: the tame robin we stop to admire while digging a border; the inquisitive blue tit that comes to investigate the new nest box you've just put up (see pages 160–65).

While there are many ways to attract birds to your garden, one project that will really draw them in with the promise of food and shelter is a coppice belt. Coppicing – an ancient tradition, most often carried out in managed woodlands – involves cutting down trees to a stump or a "stool", just above ground level. This drastic chop (done in December to March) allows light onto the woodland floor and promotes dense new growth.

We've been experimenting with coppicing for many years, and have found that a coppice is most effective when planted in a linear "belt";

A coppice provides excellent cover
and feeding opportunities for birds,
including coal tits (above) and
house sparrows (below).

We positioned canes around these existing trees to plan out where we were going to plant new specimens for the coppice.

We plant coppices fairly sparsely, to give individual trees and shrubs more of a chance to flower and produce fruit as they establish themselves.

This image, taken two years after the coppice was planted, shows how quickly the trees and shrubs have grown. A row of pendulous sedge, which we planted beneath the trees to keep creeping thistle at bay, adds to the dense, bird-friendly habitat.

for instance, as a boundary. Birds use these belts as natural corridors, with the cover of the dense branches sheltering them as they move from one area of the garden to the next. A well-planned coppice area also provides a healthy food supply to a diverse range of species (both avian and otherwise) year after year.

WHAT TO PLANT

The key to a good coppice belt is diversity. Choose a range of five or more native trees and shrubs (see pages 182–86) that differ in both growth habit and vigour: for example, a combination of birch trees grown above shrubby hazel would mimic a natural tree pairing in native woodland. Remember to keep in mind the overall spread of plants you can fit into your proposed coppice area (see below). Height is not as much of an issue as in other projects, however, since the coppicing process involves cutting your chosen trees down to a manageable height every four to seven years (see pages 38–39). If space really is at a premium, you can choose shrubs over trees if you prefer, and keep them cut back to below fence height.

HOW TO MAKE IT

Start by measuring the area you want to coppice. The minimum amount of space you'll need is around 5sq m (54sq ft); in that area you can fit five trees or shrubs, spaced out at 2m (6½ft) intervals.

It's best to plant out your chosen trees and shrubs between late November and mid-March. We recommend bare-root specimens, as these are cheaper than pot-grown plants, but whichever you choose, the planting is the same. For each plant, measure the diameter of the roots, then dig a square hole slightly larger than this diameter, and a little deeper than the depth of the roots. Remove any large stones and debris from the hole, then loosen the soil at the bottom with a

YOU COULD PLANT...

ALDER TREE

ALDER OR COMMON BUCKTHORN

ASH

ASPEN

ELM

GOAT WILLOW

GUELDER ROSE

HAZEL

HOLLY

ROWAN

SILVER BIRCH

SPINDLE

WILD CHERRY

Wood mice are great climbers and can often be spotted
in large shrubs in coppices and hedgerows.

spade or fork. Mix in a little mulch or manure, then place the plant inside,
ensuring that the soil level mark on the stem is level with the ground.
Carefully backfill around the roots with soil, then use your heels to firm the
soil around the plant.

It is best to plant the coppice in two slightly staggered rows. Choose
a somewhat larger variety for every fourth plant in each row. Opt for
multi-stemmed specimens in the back row, such as birch, wild cherry, and
rowan. Plant species such as holly, guelder rose, and spindle in the front
row to help create a good density of cover and provide birds with plenty of
shelter from strong winds and predators.

WHO LIVES THERE

The most obvious inhabitants in a coppice belt are the birds. Some species, including siskins and redpolls, will flock to enjoy the berries and seeds provided by the diverse mix of tree or shrub species, while others – such as warblers – will take advantage of the various insect larvae that they'll uncover among the coppice's branches. As for the insects that aren't snapped up by a warbler's beak, look out for the spectacular puss moth larvae (or caterpillars) on aspen and goat willow, and those of the birch sawfly on silver birch.

As the coppice belt develops, the ground beneath will collect a layer of leaf litter and twigs shed naturally from the trees and shrubs, which in turn will attract an assortment of mammals, reptiles, and amphibians.

YOU COULD HELP...

BIRCH SAWFLY MOTH

BLACKCAP

BRIMSTONE BUTTERFLY

BULLFINCH

CHIFFCHAFF

COMMON PIPISTRELLE

GARDEN WARBLER

HEDGEHOG

LONG-TAILED TIT

PUSS MOTH

REDPOLL

SISKIN

HOW TO MAINTAIN IT

Coppice belts require no management for the first three to five years; simply leave your trees or shrubs to grow and establish themselves on your plot.

Once the tallest trees or shrubs have reached your preferred height, it's time to start coppicing. Between December and March, cut down around a fifth of the trees or shrubs on your plot, leaving stumps no more than 5–7.5cm (2–3in) above ground level. After a few months, in spring, the stumps will begin to regenerate and put out new branches. Repeat this process every winter thereafter, cutting down another fifth of your trees or shrubs; this will ensure that there is always a healthy and dynamic balance of more mature growth and freshly regenerating younger growth.

If you have the space to do so, you may wish to leave the occasional tree to grow into a mature specimen. This creates a good arrival platform for birds, before they work their way down into the attractive mass of branches below.

Turn a sterile boundary into a
thriving habitat for birds and
insects – without taking up huge
amounts of space in your garden.

A WILD FENCE

It would be fair to say that, for the majority of us, fences are pretty plain. A
typical setup in an average garden is a wooden fence, erected to a height
of around 1.8m (6ft), often with some kind of gravel board or kickboard at
the bottom of the fence, in contact with the ground. But, regardless of
what they're made of (be it wood, metal, featheredge boards, or heavy-
duty trellis), fences are usually thought of as a line that simply states where
one garden finishes and the next starts. In many areas, you only have to
look out of a first-floor window to understand just how obsessed we are
with neat boundaries. Rows and rows of gardens, all tidily boxed in with
fencing, keeping homeowners in and neighbours – and wildlife – out.

If we had our way, we would remove all fences across the nation and
replace them with hedges (see pages 32–39). If we had more of these
natural wildlife corridors, the benefits for our wildlife would be huge –
providing food, shelter, and nesting potential for everything from beetles

Making use of your vertical space, as in
this garden, will maximize the wildlife
potential of your green space.

to bullfinches. That said, a hedge isn't always the most practical option, especially if you prize year-round privacy or need to keep out a neighbour's dog. There's also the issue of space to consider – not all of us are blessed with a garden large enough to accommodate hedging. So, if you do need to go down the fencing route, why not break the mould and transform a normally sterile vertical barrier into a living green oasis – without annoying the neighbours?

HOW TO MAKE IT

The secret to creating a wildlife-friendly fence is surprisingly simple: you need to put up two rows of fencing instead of one. The first row, which borders the neighbour's property, should be a standard featheredge fence. This will make sure that the neighbour's side of the boundary remains neat and tidy. If you already have a good fence in place, you're halfway there. If not, you'll need to install one (you'll find plenty of useful information about erecting fences online).

If you're constructing a new fence, install wooden gravel boards or kickboards at the base of the featheredge. Cut several square holes, approximately 12.5 x 12.5cm (5 x 5in) in size, into these boards at different points along the run of fencing. These holes will allow hedgehogs easy access in and out of your garden, while being small enough to keep out cats and dogs. Likewise, if you are hanging a gate, take care to leave enough space at the bottom for wildlife to pass beneath.

Once you're happy with your new boundary, build a second layer of fencing – this time with heavy-duty trellis. First, space your trellis away from the fence by securing some wooden blocks, around 10cm (4in) thick, at equal distances along the top and bottom of the featheredge. Screw the trellis into these blocks. This will produce a cavity between the two fences, ready for wildlife to explore in time.

YOU COULD PLANT...

DOG ROSE

FIELD ROSE

HOPS

IVY

JASMINE

PYRACANTHA

THORNLESS BRAMBLE

WILD CLEMATIS

WILD HONEYSUCKLE

For this garden project, our client wanted a wild garden, but their neighbour preferred having a smart timber fence. The result was this wildlife-friendly design.

We inserted a few bird boxes at intervals along the fence to give birds even more encouragement to make our client's garden their home.

When space is limited, we need to think creatively. The trellis slotted neatly behind a pond and compost bin, leaving plenty of room for the flowering lawn.

This photo, taken 18 months later, shows the wild fence in all its glory, with climbers flourishing across the trellis and plenty of gaps for wildlife to explore.

WHAT TO PLANT

When it comes to planting up an outdoor space, it's quite easy to concentrate on the "flat" options: lawns, meadows, borders, and so on. With a trellis, however, you're able to make the most of the vertical space in your garden. Climbers can provide a huge amount of greenery relative to their planting footprint (making them an ideal choice for small gardens), helping to boost your plot's potential to support wildlife. Plant them in spring or autumn.

For the most part we recommend choosing a range of native climbers. Wild honeysuckle is a real must-have species: its heavily scented flowers attract wonderful hawkmoths, while birds and butterflies feed on its ripe berries. Hops, more commonly known as the crop used to produce beer, is a vital species for supporting the comma butterfly, the larvae of which feed on the leaves – though do be warned, it is a fast-growing plant that can cover an entire fence in no time if left unpruned. Then there's ivy. Often (wrongly) discouraged by many because of its tendency to grow through fences, if left to mature, ivy will flower in late summer, offering a source of late-season nectar for many pollinators. Its berries provide much-needed food for birds during the winter and are the larval food for the caterpillars of the second brood of holly blue butterflies.

While native plants are preferable, we do have a few non-natives that we recommend for this project. Pyracantha is a wonderfully adaptable species, growing well in sun and shade; its dense, thorny foliage provides cover for nesting birds, who also enjoy the plant's excellent crop of berries. Jasmine, another non-native, also provides dense cover, while the availability of summer- and winter-flowering varieties means that they can be used to provide nectar throughout the seasons.

WHO LIVES THERE

Once the climbers have established themselves, the gap between the fence and the trellis will mimic the shelter provided by a hedge, making it desirable for the likes of hedgehogs as well as a range of birds. If you like, you can make the space even more appealing to birds by creating nesting spaces for them: simple shelves (made from offcuts of gravel board) will suffice for blackbirds looking to build their scruffy nests, while specially

A The caterpillar of the comma butterfly. **B** Hedgehogs love to snuffle through the undergrowth of a wild fence.

designed "roosting pockets" (made from natural materials), upturned stovetop kettles, and toe-cap boots are all fantastic for roosting wrens and robins. Hedgehogs need access to a variety of gardens in order to sustain their diet of slugs, worms, beetles, and snails, so the more gardens they can access, the greater the chance they have of finding enough food to eat.

YOU COULD HELP...

BLACKBIRD

COMMA BUTTERFLY

HAWKMOTHS

HEDGEHOG

HOLLY BLUE BUTTERFLY

ROBIN

WREN

LOOKING AFTER A WILD FENCE

Your wild fence should require minimal maintenance. Water the plants well and add mulch to the base of climbers in their first season, and within weeks the trellis will start to look greener and become more attractive to wildlife. Treat your new wild fence similar to a hedge once it has established and covered the desired area of fencing by pruning it back in late winter, before the birds start nesting.

Plant a variety of shrubs and you'll provide year-round support for a range of creatures, including birds and butterflies.

CHOOSE SHRUBS FOR WILDLIFE

Shrubs have long been a garden mainstay, and it's easy to understand why. Many species offer stunning foliage or striking stem colours, while others provide wonderfully scented flowers. Shrubs can be used to screen off certain parts of the garden, hiding an old shed from view, or they might be used as a boundary; larger shrubs can be used as hedges (see pages 32–39), while smaller varieties may be used to divide and distinguish different areas of a large garden. Often, shrubs are simply used to fill the backs of borders, a practice so ingrained in horticulture that many of us would not know what else to do with these spaces.

As far as we're concerned, a shrub's best asset is not its visual or structural appeal, but its ability to attract and support wildlife. As with any element in a garden – be it a lawn, fence, water feature, or path – shrubs have the potential to encourage biodiversity. With a little understanding of what garden visitors want from your shrubs, you can choose species that will not only suit your needs, but theirs, too.

SHRUBS FOR BIRDS

Shrubs will naturally attract birds, regardless of the species' size, shape, or colour. They offer shelter from predators, a place to nest, and plenty of food, be it from berries in the autumn and winter, or from resident and visiting insects that in turn feast on the shrubs' leaves and nectar in the warmer months. But, while most shrubs will appeal to birds, there are ways to boost a garden's ability to support avian life simply by choosing a good mix of particularly effective species.

As we've mentioned elsewhere, native species should take priority over non-natives wherever possible. You may be familiar with conifers: evergreen shrubs, such as leylandii, that are often used to create large, single-species hedges. Conifers are a classic example of a non-native shrub species, and are regularly visited by woodpigeons, blackbirds, and song thrushes to raise their young. If, however, you opt for native shrubs, such as hawthorn or holly, instead of non-natives like leylandii, you can provide equally attractive conditions for those same birds, and at the same time benefit additional species, such as the house sparrow, blue tit, and long-tailed tit, who feed on invertebrates that can only be supported by native species.

This steep bank was planted with young gorse shrubs in order to create a specialized habitat for yellowhammers and other ground-nesting birds.

Within just 18 months, the gorse grew to cover the whole bank, providing shelter for the area's resident yellowhammers, which bred the following year.

A Song thrush settled on some ivy. **B** Juvenile blue tit in a coppiced silver birch shrub. **C** A red admiral butterfly feeding on buddleja nectar. **D** A peppered moth larva well-camouflaged against a hawthorn stem.

One native species worth a particular mention when it comes to supporting birdlife is common gorse. Many of us are familiar with this scrubby shrub, which spreads across heath and moorland with ease, its yellow flowers blazing gold across the landscape. But it is virtually never considered as a garden shrub, primarily due to its invasive and thorny habit. However, if you have a bit of space (say, for instance, a scruffy and relatively undisturbed corner of your plot), this shrub provides ideal conditions for nesting birds.

On page 53, we have a before-and-after of a garden we created in North Yorkshire, which contained a steep bank of heavy clay soil left over from a wildlife pond that had previously been installed. Creeping thistles were about the only plant coping with the difficult conditions, so we cleared these away and planted gorse in 9cm (3½in) pots. In just 18 months, the gorse spread rapidly, creating a vital habitat designed to appeal to yellowhammers and linnets. By the third year, yellowhammers did breed in the dense thicket, which was a great success.

C

D

For scrubby shrubs like gorse, an occasional cut back every now and again in winter is all that is needed in terms of management. They may not look quite as neat as the likes of a perfectly pruned leylandii, but by thinking about shrubs differently – in other words, considering how they would grow in the wild, rather than how they've traditionally been used in a garden context – you will definitely attract more birds into your plot.

SHRUBS FOR BUTTERFLIES

When it comes to attracting butterflies to a garden, we first tend to consider nectar-rich plants (see pages 92–111), followed by the likes of wildflowers (see pages 112–47), but alongside all of this vital planting we shouldn't forget about shrubs. Not only do certain butterflies feed on the nectar provided by various flowering shrubs, but some species can only lay their eggs on native shrubs, and need them to complete their life cycle.

Brimstone caterpillars often pupate on the shrubs they
once fed upon, as with this alder buckthorn.

If any shrub is known for attracting butterflies, it's buddleja. Also known as
the "butterfly bush", the shrub, with its purple, yellow, lilac, or white flowers,
can often be seen growing naturally on waste land or along railway lines,
and is an excellent choice for a wild garden. Simply plant it in a sunny,
sheltered spot and give it a hard prune around late March or early April; this
will ensure that it flowers later in summer when the nectar is needed most.

VARIETY IS KEY

We've already highlighted a couple of our favourite shrubs for attracting
wildlife, but in truth, there are dozens of options available. While some are
better than others, there isn't one single shrub we would recommend over
all others – and nor would we want to. As with all planting, the best way to
support the widest range of local wildlife is by choosing a diverse mix of
species, with each one bringing something different to your plot. If you
can, try to include enough varieties that your garden will provide a source
of food throughout the year, be it berries, flowers, or foliage.

If this feels like a daunting task, below we've highlighted a few of our favourites to get you started. Each of these shrubs offer multiple benefits: some support multiple species throughout the seasons, while others are notable for providing valuable berries when other food sources are scarce. You can also turn to the Plant Lists on pages 182–86 to find a full list of species to choose from.

The species you choose to include on your garden, and what you do with them, is up to you. You can space them around the plot, or group them to create a hedge (see pages 32–39) or small coppice belt (see pages 40–45). Whatever you decide, the key is to grow your shrubs in a sheltered environment, with as much sun and as little wind as possible.

A FEW OF OUR FAVOURITES

Holly's dense, evergreen foliage provides ideal nesting opportunities for many birds, while its red berries are a vital source of food during the winter months. Come spring, the shrub also hosts the first brood of the holly blue butterfly, which lays its eggs on the shrub's flowers.

Hawthorn is another excellent species that provides plenty of berries in autumn, as well as good winter shelter. It's one of the best shrubs you can grow to support insects, too: it attracts more than 300 species!

Elder, probably our most neglected native shrub, is an exceptionally good plant that provides late summer berries for a range of bird species including blackcap, whitethroat, and lesser whitethroat.

Then there is alder buckthorn, which is a must-have shrub for any garden given its appeal to the brimstone butterfly, which lays its eggs on the foliage. While it prefers damper soils (especially acid and neutral soils), we've had success growing it in average garden topsoil.

Dogwood is worth a mention, too. Popular with gardeners for providing beautiful winter stem colour, this shrub species also provides a good number of berries in autumn for garden visitors. Holly blue and green hairstreak butterflies lay their eggs on the plant in spring.

Finally, you have wild privet, a semi-evergreen shrub that naturally grows in woodland habitats, where it is a favourite of the rare black hairstreak butterflies. While you may not attract this species to your garden, you may be visited by speckled wood butterflies, who feed on wild privet nectar.

WILDLIFE PONDS

Nothing beats a pond when it comes to attracting and supporting wildlife. No matter the size of your outdoor space, every gardener should have a water feature on their plot.

INTRODUCTION

We regularly get asked the same question: If you could do only one thing to attract wildlife into your garden, what would it be? Our answer is simple: create a pond.

By definition, a freshwater pond is a body of water anywhere between 1 sq metre (11sq ft) and 2 hectares (5 acres) in size that holds water for at least four months of the year. With this in mind, it's no surprise that ponds and their associated habitats come in a vast and complex array of shapes and sizes – be it a natural depression created by a fallen tree's root plate, an ancient river oxbow, or a formal pool in a city centre.

Like so many of our wild places, though, there has been a drastic decline in good-quality ponds in the wider countryside. At least half of the UK's ponds were lost during the twentieth century, and most of those that remain are in a sad state. The reasons for these losses are many: ponds have been simply abandoned and silted up, been infilled on farmland when no longer needed, and in urban areas they've been neglected to the point of abandonment through something as simple as littering.

> If you could do only
> one thing to attract
> wildlife to your garden,
> create a pond.

In the UK, it's incredible to think that two-thirds of all freshwater species are supported by ponds. For that reason alone, they are worth preserving and creating – not that you should ever need an excuse to make such a wonderful habitat for wildlife!

Wherever you live, having a wildlife pond in your own garden brings so many delights, whether you want to hear the humble common frog croaking away in early spring, watch the dragon-like shapes of great crested newts emerging from the depths, or sit surrounded by dragonflies, patrolling for any passing insects.

A natural pond will be a great addition to any wildlife garden. If you are landscaping around your property, you may wish to create a stylish formal pool. A small container pond could be a solution if you are faced with limited space in your garden. Whatever you wish to do, the following pages will guide you through the process of designing, creating, and maintaining your mini wetland.

Water really is the key to life, and by planning your pond properly, you will have a garden full of dragonflies, bathing birds, and amphibians in no time.

A good pond is the heart of any wild garden – a place where you can spend hours enjoying the unfolding dramas of freshwater life.

A NATURAL POND

When it comes to attracting wildlife into a garden, there is no better project to undertake than creating a simple pond. While the other projects in this book might appeal to specific creatures, a pond will support everything; after all, even the smallest bee needs a drink now and then.

PLANNING YOUR POND

When planning where to site your pond, locate it away from trees and large shrubs where heavy shade, roots, leaves, and potential falling debris are likely to cause future problems. Consider also the position of any underground pipes and cables before you start to dig.

If you can, site the pond in a naturally low part of the plot, as this will collect rainwater and be more sheltered from the wind. It ideally needs to be a sunny spot, too (see pages 14–15).

With easy access and plenty of planting around the margins, this natural pond appeals to a range of garden visitors.

Make the pond as large as your space and budget will allow. Ponds are so much easier to look after when they are larger, with slower rates of water loss, and can therefore withstand severe drought for much longer than a smaller, shallower pond.

Using a garden hose or some string, mark out the outline of the pond. Keep the outline as natural as possible, with no awkward angles and tight corners, as these can make lining the pond difficult.

DIGGING YOUR POND

Once you are happy with the size and shape of your pond, you can start digging. If your pond is under 6sq m (65sq ft) in size, digging by hand is perfectly achievable; for this you'll need a strong spade, a shovel, and a pickaxe. If you are considering a much larger pond, it is definitely worth hiring a mini-digger and an experienced contractor to operate it.

If there is any turf to remove, strip this off first and set it aside, then start to dig. It makes sense to begin digging where you intend to have the deepest part of the pond. Wildlife ponds up to 6sq m (65sq ft) should have a minimum depth of 60–90cm (2–3ft); for larger ponds, aim for a minimum depth of around 90–120cm (3–4ft). Deep water provides a refuge for species through the winter months.

After you have reached the deepest point of the pond, you can simply dig your way outwards, taking less depth out as you near the pond margins to create gently sloping sides.

Don't throw away the turf and topsoil you dig up. With a little planning, even these "waste" products from the creation of your pond can be utilized and made into brilliant habitats in their own right. You can, for instance, use them to create a wildflower bank (see pages 104–11). We often incorporate old logs, stones, and rubble into these banks to create excellent hibernation sites for amphibians and reptiles.

Depending on your location, you may find that the soil begins to change colour and texture as you dig deeper. This paler soil, known as subsoil, is invaluable to the creation of a wildlife pond (as we'll explain in a moment). Any subsoil that is relatively workable and free of sharp stones and debris should be retained near the pond, as it will come in very useful later on.

Wait until the pond is filled to its final level before planting marginal species, such as brooklime and water avens, along the water's edge.

A shallow, pebble-covered beach area helps to keep a section of the pond free from vegetation, allowing birds to access the water in order to bathe and drink.

No natural wildlife pond would be complete without the addition of a "dragonfly perch" (see page 70). As well as appealing to dragonflies, the feature will also attract birds – the great tits and house sparrows in the image above seem to really enjoy it!

LINING THE POND

When you've finished digging out the pond and are happy with its internal shape (known as its profile), use a spirit level to make sure that the outer margins are all an even height. Check that there are no sharp objects on the soil's surface that could cause potential damage to the liner material, then put down down a layer of underlay fleece. Smooth this out over the profile as best as you can, making sure that there are no large folds anywhere.

Next, it's time to install the pond liner. The simplest and most reliable lining material for garden ponds is a flexible synthetic lining, such as PVC. This is a good, cost-effective liner that will last many years with careful installation. The next step up from PVC are EDPM and butyl rubber liners. Both are costlier, but offer tough puncture resistance and many years of reliable service. We use 1mm- (1/32in-) thick butyl rubber liners for all our pond installations, but our best advice is simply to purchase the best you can with your available budget. At the end of the day, a pond is completely dependent on being able to hold water in the first place!

With a helper or two, unfold or roll out the pond liner to fully cover the fleece-lined hole. Now, take your time here. Remove your boots (to protect the liner), carefully walk towards the lowest point of the pond, and begin to smooth out the liner with your hands from the bottom, working your way up and out of the hole. You may well find that you have to work a few folds into one or more large, neat folds as you go.

Once the liner fits neatly into the hole, put your boots back on and place another layer of fleece on top. This ensures that the liner is extremely well protected from above. Remember to leave both the liner and the fleece untrimmed around the pond margins for the moment.

The next stage is key to creating a really good wildlife pond: it's time to bring in the subsoil you set aside earlier. Subsoil is a low-nutrient aggregate that will not only give your pond a fantastic natural look, but will also form an ideal growing medium for your pond plants, meaning that you won't have to rely on unsightly and restrictive planting baskets.

An effective subsoil layer should be around 75–100mm (3–4in) thick. If you managed to dig up enough subsoil for this layer, great. If not, you can excavate extra from elsewhere in your plot, enquire with local quarries and aggregate suppliers or, if need be, cover the fleece with a layer of stones, pebbles, cobbles, or gravel. Never use normal, nutrient-rich topsoil, as this will cause all manner of problems, including excessive algal growth and generally unhealthy water conditions. Spread the subsoil over the fleece, starting from the bottom of the pond and slowly working up the sides. Walk over the whole area to compact the soil, then climb out of the hole and lightly rake the surface so that no boot prints remain visible.

Finally, create a "beach" area. This will provide animals with a good access point in and out of the water, a space for birds to bathe and drink, and ideal conditions for tadpoles to develop. Choose a wide, shallow side of your pond and place a few large, heavy stones beneath the water line to support the weight of the beach above. Then, working up and out of the hole, set down a layer of smaller pebbles and stones, until you're happy with the beach's size and appearance.

FILLING THE POND

Finally, you're ready to add water. Rainwater is best, but since we don't often have access to hundreds of litres of it, simply fill the pond with water from the mains if need be. Don't feel guilty about this. Almost every wildlife pond we have created has been filled with tap water. The chlorine will soon disperse, and although tap water contains significantly more nutrients than rainwater, plants will use these up in time. In the future, you might want to consider installing a couple of water butts, to ensure you have a ready supply of rainwater to refill your pond during drier spells.

Rainwater is best to fill your wildlife pond, but tap water works fine, too.

If using a hose to fill the hole with water, place an offcut of liner or fleece beneath the nozzle before you turn on the tap. This will prevent the strong jet of water from eroding the soil and clouding the pond. Once the pond is almost filled and you know exactly where the finished water level will sit, trim away any excess liner or fleece and cover the raw edges with subsoil.

WHAT TO PLANT

You can dig and plant your pond at almost any time of the year, but the best time to do it is between May and July, when aquatic plants grow most strongly and the water is warm; many plant species simply don't grow between August and April.

As with planting any part of a wildlife garden, variety is key. Choose at least three different types of pond plants from each category in the list (see pages 182–86). You can purchase them either in 9cm (3½in) pots or as plugs. We recommend plugs, as these tend to be more cost-effective, grow very quickly, and are easier to plant directly into the subsoil.

Plant your specimens directly into the subsoil while the pond is filling, taking care not to damage the liner with any tools you are using. It's a good idea to position taller species towards the rear of the pond, so your views across the water aren't restricted.

Once you have finished adding your pond plants, sow a "water's edge" or "wetland" seed mixture of fine grasses and additional aquatic species around the margins. The seeds should germinate within a few weeks, and before long will fill in any patches of bare soil around your new pond and provide cover for amphibians, particularly young frogs and toads that need damp places to hide when leaving the water.

YOU COULD PLANT...

BROOKLIME

CUCKOOFLOWER

FRINGED WATER LILY

GREATER BIRD'S-FOOT TREFOIL

HARD RUSH

HORNWORT

PURPLE LOOSESTRIFE

RAGGED ROBIN

WATER MINT

WHO LIVES THERE

It is remarkable how rapidly a well-made wildlife pond can establish itself. Within just a few months, it is possible to have a freshwater habitat that is teeming with life, from water snails and shrimps to dragonfly larvae and newts. While any source of freshwater will be a haven for local species, there are a few extra elements you can add to your pond to really bring it to life. One

A Gatekeeper butterfly on common fleabane **B** Purple loosestrife
C Fringed water lily and water soldier **D** Greater bird's-foot trefoil

A Blue-tailed damselfly B Frogspawn
C Water boatman D Common frog

simple addition we recommend is to place a couple of pieces of rotten wood (ideally from a native tree) along the water's edge so that they are half-submerged beneath the water. These will be highly desirable to both brown hawker and southern hawker dragonflies for laying their eggs on. You can also offer young amphibians a safe refuge by adding a few log piles, rocks, and pieces of bark around the pond.

Another really good finishing touch is a dragonfly perch. Find a sturdy branch that tapers to a thin point, and fix this so it overhangs the water. It will prove irresistible to dragonflies and damselflies throughout the spring and summer months, and the birds will love perching on it too.

LOOKING AFTER YOUR POND

Managing a wildlife pond is relatively easy. Your main priority in the first year will be protecting it from any damage (particularly to the subsoil layer), which could be caused by people or dogs stepping onto the pond margins. Don't be tempted to add any fish, as this can be detrimental to any other species trying to become established.

C

D

YOU COULD HELP...

BROAD-BODIED CHASER

COMMON FROG

FRESHWATER SHRIMP

GRASS SNAKE

LARGE RED DAMSELFLY

RAMSHORN SNAIL

SMOOTH NEWT

WATER SCORPION

WATER SPIDER

WHIRLIGIG BEETLE

During the first year, you will also need to gently remove any blanket weed (green algae) from the surface of the water with a pond net or rake. This will be less of a problem as time goes on; once species such as fringed water lily and broad-leaved pondweed grow to cover a large percentage of the water's surface (usually around 80 per cent), the blanket weed should disappear. You should also keep an eye on the water level, particularly during the summer, and top it up as needed (especially if it drops below half).

From around the second year onwards, you may need to remove excess vegetation (more than 80 per cent). The best time to do this is the end of summer, before autumn really sets in. Any vegetation you remove from the water should be left on the margins for a day to allow pond creatures time to return to the water if they have accidentally been removed from the pond.

With a little careful planning,
wildlife gardening and good
design can combine to create
a wonderfully diverse habitat.

A FORMAL POND

If we're going to install a water feature immediately next to a house, or in public spaces such as a hospital garden or school grounds where safe and stable hard surfaces are essential, a formal pond can often be the most practical option available to us.

A formal pond, with its hard-landscaped outline and often steep sides, can be lethal for animals such as hedgehogs – simply put, once they fall in, they can't climb out. But, by taking the time to consider how wildlife will use the pond alongside your own perspective, you can design and create a formal water feature that will allow all manner of creatures to thrive there.

In this project we'll show you how to transform an existing formal water feature into a wildlife haven, and ways to design a wildlife-friendly formal pond if you're planning to have a brand-new one installed in your garden.

This formal pond contains a wildlife-
friendly secret: two shallow access
shelves submerged beneath the water.

REWILDING EXISTING FORMAL PONDS

A newt doesn't care if a pond is surrounded by paving slabs. It cares about whether it can get in and out of the water easily and if there is sufficient cover in the margins to hide in and where females can lay eggs. So, if you have an existing formal water feature, take a moment to think about it from a newt's point of view, and see what can be done to make things a little easier for it and other visiting creatures. This is an essential aspect of any wildlife pond, but especially for steep-sided formal ponds that offer little to no purchase for animals that need to climb out of the water.

A simple solution to any access issues is to create an easy route in and out of the water via the addition of items such as rotten wood, cobbles, sticks, and logs. These extras may look a little out of place along the neat edges of the pond, but your visitors will thank you for them.

If your pond is not planted up, use aquatic baskets to provide some much-needed vegetation. These allow you to add plants to your existing water feature without having to worry about putting down a layer of subsoil. Aquatic baskets come in all shapes and sizes, and can be bought online or from most garden centres; alternatively, you could reuse any old plastic baskets you might have going spare. Pour a layer of aquatic compost into the base of the baskets, add your plants (see page 78), then top the compost with some grit or gravel to prevent the compost from floating out of the basket. Carefully place the baskets into the pond (you may need a hook-ended pole to do this), and before you know it, your old pond will provide plenty of cover and shade for wildlife.

DESIGNING A NEW FORMAL POND

Unless you have some experience with bricklaying and handling concrete, we would recommend hiring a professional landscaping company to install a formal pond from scratch (see page 192), as it requires more technical knowledge and specialist equipment than a simple natural pond. But,

A 'Candida' water lilies B Hostas
C Soft shield fern D Purple loosestrife

while you may not need to roll your sleeves up for this project, there are still some things you should keep in mind while you plan and design your pond.

One of the most obvious differences between a natural pond and a formal pond is its shape: instead of the wilder, more random shapes we normally associate with wildlife ponds, a typical formal pond design will incorporate straight lines and smooth surfaces. The pond's outline can be whatever shape you like – if you want a perfect circle or a neat rectangle, go ahead. What you do need to do, though, is be sure to contour the bottom of the pond in a wildlife-friendly way. Unlike the bottom of a typical natural pond, which might resemble something like a gently sloping pudding bowl or dish, with a formal pond you're more likely to want a flat base. When we install a new formal pond, we include wide, flat shelves around the perimeter (see opposite). These sit just below the water line once the pond is filled, and can support a good amount of planting baskets if you are not planning on adding a layer of subsoil (see pages 66–67).

We also recommend including at least one gently sloping margin where animals can enter and exit safely. The shallower water will also stay slightly warmer than the rest of the pond, which will be beneficial to amphibians and invertebrate larvae that prefer such conditions to develop in.

Another element you might want to include in your formal pond design is flowing water. This is simply a matter of personal choice. Most freshwater pond plants can thrive in moving water, as long as the flow is relatively slow. Alternatively, if you simply wish to hear the sound of gently flowing water, consider installing a small, gently trickling bubble fountain.

> If your pond has steep sides, prop logs against the edge to provide wildlife with safe access in and out of the water.

WHAT TO PLANT

The planting of a formal pond can be similar to that of a natural one (see page 69), although it is also a great opportunity to include some more ornamental additions, such as lilies, Siberian iris, and any varieties of colourful primulas that

To achieve a formal outline, we built this rectangular pond using breeze blocks. For a project this large you may need to hire professionals to realize your design.

We included two shallow shelves around the pond's edge to create an area for planting while also providing wildlife with an easy-to-reach access platform.

A row of lush pond plants were positioned along the shelf on the far side of the pond to provide a habitat for wildlife – as well as plenty of visual interest for human visitors.

This water feature pours into a second pool, separate yet connected to the main pond, so that the owner could enjoy the sound without any pond plants or creatures being disturbed by the flow.

A Common carder bee and purple loosestrife
B Four-spotted chaser dragonfly **C** A pair of large
red damselflies mating **D** Common frog

thrive in bog conditions. Whatever plants you choose, make sure to incorporate a good mix of all types of aquatic plant, including marginals, oxygenators, emergents, and floating-leaved species (see pages 182–86).

You can add subsoil to a formal pond the way you would with a natural one (see pages 66–67), as it won't affect water clarity. However, if you would prefer not to do this, you can still achieve a healthy and good-looking pond by using quality aquatic baskets and compost, as discussed on page 75. Aim for dense, well-planted margins, and add a good number of strategically placed stones and logs to provide good access in and out of the water.

WHAT TO PLANT...

ARROWHEAD

BROAD-LEAVED POND WEED

BROOK LIME

COMMON FLEABANE

FRINGED WATER LILY

HARD RUSH

LESSER POND SEDGE

PURPLE LOOSESTRIFE

WATER AVENS

WATER MINT

WATER PLANTAIN

YELLOW FLAG IRIS

C

D

WHO LIVES THERE

The main characters that you can expect to find in your formal pond will be much the same as a natural pond, although you may spot more toads, as as they prefer deeper water, ideally around 1.2m (4ft) deep. If access to the water's edge is good, you may also spot foxes and hedgehogs stopping by your pond to drink.

LOOKING AFTER YOUR POND

Maintaining a formal pond will generally follow the same advice provided on pages 70–71. Just make sure to check access points regularly to be sure that your pond visitors continue to have easy access in and out of the water.

YOU COULD HELP...

BADGER

BLACKBIRD

BLUE-TAILED DAMSELFLY

COLLARED DOVE

COMMON BLUE DAMSELFLY

COMMON FROG

FOUR-SPOTTED CHASER DRAGONFLY

FOX

GREAT CRESTED NEWT

HEDGEHOG

HOUSE SPARROW

SMOOTH NEWT

Bogs are unassuming but miraculous places. Create your own and it will be teeming with life in no time.

A BOG GARDEN

A bog is any piece of land highly saturated with water. In the wild, nature's bogs are peat bogs. These unique and rich wildlife habitats are also invaluable "carbon sinks", meaning that they absorb and store carbon, keeping it out of the atmosphere. We hear a lot about the importance of trees in the fight against climate change, but not nearly enough about peat bogs, which capture twice as much carbon as all standing forests. Plus, they filter water and help to reduce the risk of flooding.

And yet, in spite of all these benefits, the state of bogs across the UK and elsewhere is a source of huge concern. On agricultural land, bogs are disappearing due to sophisticated drainage techniques, while the relentless sale of peat-based compost in garden centres continues to strip vast tracts of peat bog bare at an alarming rate, degrading these ancient wild landscapes and releasing stored carbon in the process.

For many gardeners, a wet corner can be a problem. Embrace the ground's bogginess for your own slice of wetland.

Although you can't exactly replicate these precious habitats in your own garden, you can create a mini-bog garden that will act as a wonderful damp sanctuary for a fascinating array of plants and animals.

CREATING YOUR BOG GARDEN

If you already have a pond or are planning to dig one (see pages 64–67), you can situate a bog garden immediately next to it. The bog will collect any overflowing water and be an amazing wildlife habitat in its own right. That said, you don't need a pond to have a bog garden. It can be a completely separate, standalone feature; all that matters is that you ensure the soil stays saturated with water and doesn't dry out.

The location of your bog isn't too critical, although siting it in a low-lying area will help it collect and retain water for longer. A sunny spot will give you more planting options, but a number of pond plants can be used in shady situations, too.

If you plan to site your bog next to a pond, find the lowest point of the pond's margins – the spot where any excess rainwater will naturally flow out of the pond first. To put it another way, if your pond is situated on a slight slope, site the bog on the downhill side. If your pond margins are all level, you can locate the bog anywhere you wish.

To create the bog, dig a steep-sided, bowl-shaped hole around 30–45cm (12–18in) deep at its lowest point. Ensure that the edges of the hole are fairly level. Line the hole with fleece, pond liner, and more fleece, as you would with a natural pond (see pages 66–67). If you are connecting your

YOU COULD GROW...

BILBERRY*

BUGLE

COMMON FLEABANE

COTTON-GRASS*

CROSS-LEAVED HEATH*

CUCKOO FLOWER

DEVIL'S BIT SCABIOUS

GREATER BIRD'S-FOOT TREFOIL

HEMP AGRIMONY

PURPLE LOOSESTRIFE

PURPLE MOOR-GRASS*

RAGGED ROBIN

TANSY

YELLOW FLAG IRIS

WATER AVENS

WATER MINT

(*PEAT BOG SPECIES)

A Bugle B Greater bird's-foot trefoil
C Yellow flag iris D Cuckooflower

bog to a pond, make sure the bog's liner overlaps with the liner of the pond; this will ensure that the bog is topped up every time the pond overflows. Fill the bog with soil to a depth of at least 20–25cm (8–10in), then add a few pieces of bark, rotting logs, or even old roof tiles around the edge to attract bog-loving creatures. You should not need to fill the bog with water; by being positioned next to a pond or in a low-lying area, it should naturally fill up and remain boggy.

WHAT TO PLANT

Purchase plants as plugs (see page 69) to plant during spring or autumn. Aside from oxygenators and floating-leaved plants, almost all species on the pond plant list (see pages 182–86) will positively thrive in a bog garden. You can choose to emulate natural bogland by adding native plants, especially nectar-rich species to attract bog-loving insects. Try combining the large, robust spikes of yellow flag iris with tall stems of purple loosestrife and hemp agrimony at the back of the bog for height, with ragged robin and cuckooflower nearer the front, interspersed with hard rush for year–round cover and interest.

Alternatively, if you want to be inventive with your bog, consider recreating the more specialized habitat of a peat-style bog. Instead of subsoil, use acidic soil (or ericaceous compost) to fill the bog; this will enable you to grow some interesting and somewhat uncommon native peat bog plants, such as cross-leaved heath and the beautiful cotton-grass, alongside purple moor-grass and bilberry.

WHO LIVES THERE

Gently take a peek beneath one of those pieces of bark you placed around the bog's edge and you'll often find an assortment of young amphibians, including smooth newts and common frogs, hiding in these wonderfully damp and cool spots.

In amongst the boggy vegetation, you may spot the odd grass snake on its hunt for frogs. Your choice of bog plants will also help to attract butterflies and bees: tansy, for instance, is one of the favourite plants of the holly blue butterfly.

A Broad-bodied chaser dragonfly
B Common frog

LOOKING AFTER YOUR BOG GARDEN

Bog gardens are quite self-sufficient, requiring only minimal maintenance. The most important aspect of bog care is keeping them damp throughout dry spells with plenty of rainwater. Cut back or dig out any excess vegetation occasionally, as required. With this minimal input, you'll have a small patch of boggy sanctuary that will thrive for years to come.

YOU COULD HELP...

BROWN HAWKER DRAGONFLY

COMMON FROG

GRASS SNAKE

GREEN-VEINED WHITE BUTTERFLY

HOLLY BLUE BUTTERFLY

ORANGE TIP BUTTERFLY

SOUTHERN HAWKER DRAGONFLY

Create a mini-oasis in the smallest of spaces with the addition of a mini-pond. They're easy to make and attract a wealth of wildlife.

A CONTAINER POND

The idea of having a wildlife pond sounds great, but in reality there can be all sorts of reasons that might make it impractical, especially in small or urban gardens. The ground may be covered by a lot of hard standing or concrete, or have cables and pipes running underground. You may be living in rented accommodation, with a landlord who might not want you digging a pond in their garden. In fact, you might not even have a garden at all: for many city-dwellers nowadays, a balcony is the only outdoor space available. Or, perhaps, the idea of digging your own pond is just too daunting, either for physical or for financial reasons.

What if we told you there was a no-dig alternative that would allow you to make your own wildlife-friendly water feature? A container pond can be placed almost anywhere, and is cost-effective and simple to make, too.

The logs stacked around this mini-pond, made from an old sink, allow creatures to safely access the water's edge.

HOW TO MAKE IT

First, you'll need to find a suitable container. Something durable, preferably around 60 x 45cm (24 x 18in) in size – or 60 x 60cm (24 x 24in) if possible – with a depth of 30–40cm (12–16in). Old porcelain sinks, and stone troughs all work well, as do metal tanks. If you don't have anything like this to hand, check out websites like Freecycle, or head down to a local salvage yard. You should be able to find something suitable at a reasonably low price, or even for free if you're willing to collect the container yourself.

You can also use half barrels, which are simply old oak whisky barrels. These are sold either whole or cut in half, ready to be turned into planters – or, in this case, water features.

Double-check that the container is watertight by filling it with water and checking for leaks. There's nothing more frustrating than assembling your pond and adding plants, only to find that the water drains away five minutes after filling it up. You can use a piece of pond liner to line your container if necessary, but fitting it to small, awkward shapes can be difficult, and the results often appear messy, so it's best to avoid this if you can.

> Give an old porcelain sink, tank, or barrel a new lease of life by turning it into a mini-pond.

Next, you need to position your pond in a good spot (see pages 14–15). When you're happy with its location, it's time to think about accessibility. Some newts and frogs are capable of climbing up some surprisingly steep surfaces, but all the same it's worth creating an easy route to the pond's edge.

A simple solution is to pile up logs and pieces of bark against at least one side of the container. This will have the added benefit of creating a small habitat heap for invertebrates and amphibians to enjoy (see pages 152–55). If your pond is positioned on soil or grass, you could also pile up a mound of soil against the container to create a slope up to the lip of the pond. However, if you are using a wooden container, such as a half-barrel, be sure to wrap a waterproof membrane or pond liner over any surface that will come into contact with soil, as direct contact with damp soil may cause the timber to decay.

As well as working out a way for creatures to reach the pond, you also need to think about creating a route out of the container, so that creatures who enter the pond aren't left struggling to get a foothold on a smooth or vertical wall. A sloping pile of stones, bricks, or even rubble works well here.

If you're planning to plant up your container pond, you may need to add a couple of bricks or breeze blocks to the base of the container to ensure that the planting baskets will sit just below the water surface so they're not visible. Otherwise, it's time to fill your container. As with any other pond, rainwater is best, although if that's a little hard to come by (if you only have balcony access, for instance), tap water will suffice. (Note that there is a greater risk of blanket weed appearing if you use tap water.)

WHAT TO PLANT

Once you are happy with your additions to your container pond, and you're satisfied with the access routes, it's time to add plants. There is a range of plants suitable for growing in a container pond, as they are relatively small and will not grow to overwhelm the limited space. We recommend planting some emergent vegetation (plants that stand above the water's surface), such as purple loosestrife or hard rush, to allow insects such as dragonflies and damselflies to crawl up when they hatch into their adult forms. You could also plant some brooklime for newts to lay their eggs on, or perhaps some water mint, which might even attract the odd passing holly blue butterfly to stop for some nectar.

As with any other type of pond, you'll need to make sure you include a good balance of the different types of pond plants as shown in the pond plant list (see pages 182–86), even if you only have

YOU COULD GROW...

BROOKLIME

FROGBIT

HARD RUSH

HORNWORT*

MARSH MARIGOLD

PURPLE LOOSESTRIFE

SPIKED WATER MILFOIL*

WATER AVENS

WATER FORGET-ME-NOT

WATER MINT

WATER PLANTAIN

(*OXYGENATORS)

room for a single plant of each type. Make sure you use aquatic compost when planting up the baskets.

Choosing the right balance of oxygenators, emergent vegetation, and plants that will provide nectar for passing insects is arguably more important than a larger pond, as space is a premium and you want to make the most of what you've got. Planting the wrong type of plant (such as a flag iris) may end up with the small pond being engulfed in vegetation, leaving no open water for passing dragonflies and damselflies to lay their eggs in, or, worse still, making it harder for insects such as water boatmen to see a pond at all.

WHO LIVES THERE

In no time at all you will have an amazing amount of freshwater life visiting your mini-pond. As well as dragonflies, damselflies, and water boatmen, you may see whirligig beetles, and bees, wasps, and other flying insects coming to drink. We once converted an old porcelain sink into a mini-pond in a terraced garden, and a smooth newt turned up after just a few days.

YOU COULD HELP...

COMMON BLUE DAMSELFLY

COMMON DARTER DRAGONFLY

COMMON FROG

FOUR-SPOTTED CHASER DRAGONFLY

HOLLY BLUE BUTTERFLY

POND SKATERS

SMOOTH NEWT

WATER BOATMEN

WHIRLIGIG BEETLE

LOOKING AFTER YOUR CONTAINER POND

One of the best things about having such a small pond is that maintenance is minimal. Occasionally, you may need to remove the odd bit of blanket weed, or cut back some enthusiastic plant growth. During the summer, top up the water level from time to time as needed; with such a small volume of water in the container, this can be done quite easily. If you have room in your garden, we recommend keeping a water butt for this purpose, so that you always have a supply of rainwater to hand.

A Common toad B Dragonfly nymph casing
C Four-spotted chaser dragonfly D Water avens

NECTAR BORDERS

Reinvent the traditional garden border: by putting nectar-rich plants centre stage, you'll provide pollinating insects, including butterflies and bees, with an oasis of flowers to explore and enjoy.

INTRODUCTION

Picture a traditional suburban garden. The image that probably springs to mind is that of a neat lawn with borders around the edge. These borders may be simple, narrow, regimented rows of bedding plants, or deep, sweeping beds of exotic flowers and shrubs. Whatever form they take, herbaceous borders are the pride and joy of countless gardeners – but are far less appealing to passing pollinators, who may find few nectar-rich perennials on offer for them to enjoy.

There's nothing wrong with choosing border plants for their visual appeal, be it for their flowers, fancy foliage, or even simply their bark colour in the winter. After all, any garden with plants of some kind is always better than artificial turf and plastic topiary in pots! Nevertheless, borders have the potential to offer huge benefits to pollinating insects, provided we take a more open-minded approach to what we choose to plant.

For many years, we have been planting "nectar borders" in our clients' gardens. As their name suggests, these are borders, beds, or other spaces that are specifically designed to supply a rich supply of nectar available to pollinators when in flower. Growing plants for nectar is not a new concept,

Far too many
gardens provide
almost no sources
of nectar for
pollinators to
feed on.

but it's an uncommon practice for most gardeners. In fact, many gardens are almost sterile in terms of nectar, with virtually nothing to offer passing insects.

In this chapter, we'll show you how we go about creating a typical nectar border filled with flowering plants, as well as a more unusual project, which transforms limestone or chalk aggregate and "waste" soil into a bank of nectar-rich wildflowers and grasses. These projects may not look quite like the formal borders you might find in your neighbour's garden, but they will still be full of colourful flowers and lush foliage to catch the eye.

Of course, the core principle behind this chapter – choosing flowering plants specifically to attract and support pollinators and other insects – can be applied throughout your garden. Get creative: why not try planting shade-loving flowers under a tree, or low-growing, nectar-rich plants in the spaces between paving stones? Even a balcony could be brightened up with a few pots of wildflowers, and provide a source of nectar in the process.

Whatever you choose, it's time for us to break free from traditional ideas of high-maintenance herbaceous borders, and embrace the fact that beautiful planting can also help to support a host of nectar-loving insects.

What gardener can resist having a border full of colourful plants to enjoy – especially one designed to support pollinators?

A NECTAR BORDER

The beauty of wildlife gardening is the fact that you can be creative with the ways in which you encourage wildlife onto your plot. You don't have to follow strict rules and exact plans, like having to mow the lawn in rigid stripes or being constantly on the lookout for weeds. Instead, you can take some of the best parts of traditional gardening and turn them into features designed to attract as much wildlife as possible. Rather than having a classic herbaceous border, for instance, you could create a nectar border.

As its name suggests, a nectar border typically follows a fence, wall, or hedge and provides a ribbon of ground that's filled with colourful flowering plants. In addition to looking great, these nectar-rich flowers can really boost the number and variety of pollinating insects that spend time in your garden. Regardless of where you live, having a good source of readily available nectar is crucial for pollinators, as many often have to fly large distances looking for sustenance.

Fill your borders with nectar-rich flowering plants such as marjoram and hyssop to attract bees and butterflies.

In this garden, the border was already a patch of garlic mustard, great for the orange tip butterfly, but could be improved.

Once planted, the border became busy with passing insects all day from spring to autumn. A row of lavender along the front edge provided an attractive, formal look.

HOW TO MAKE IT

First, work out the best place to site your border. Based on your garden's aspect (see pages 14–15), find a spot that is, ideally, both sunny and sheltered, as invertebrates love sunshine. If your garden only receives limited amounts of sun, don't worry too much, as you can always opt for a selection of shade-loving species for your border (see page 100). You might also want to think about where you will spend the most time sitting in the garden, and position your border near that area. After all, you'll want to be able to enjoy the sight of both the flowers and the insects that will be visiting them.

Next, you'll need to assess your soil. Good drainage is vital for many of the best nectar plants, and most of the species we recommend for this project enjoy well-drained soil. If drainage is an issue – for instance, if you have very stony ground, hard standing such as paving slabs or concrete, or soil that stays wet all year – you could consider growing your nectar border in a raised bed. You can buy ready-made raised beds, or construct your own using some timber sleepers or gravel board. If you are planting directly into the ground, prepare the soil by digging it over and removing any roots, weeds, and stones.

> Weeds won't be a problem if you fill up every inch of space in your borders.

WHAT TO PLANT

There are two types of plant that are especially suited to this project: perennials, which live for at least a few years, growing and flowering each year, and biennials, which complete their life cycle in two years (growing foliage in the first year and flowers in the second, before setting seed and dying off). If you have the space, you could also consider planting a nectar-rich shrub or two, such as a buddleja (see page 56).

Choose a variety of different nectar-rich species from the Plant List (see pages 182–86), with the aim of having a border that will provide nectar across as many months of the year as possible. For this reason, consider planting verbena bonariensis, as it flowers from June right through to November. This herbaceous perennial is used by a wealth of insects – we've recorded more than 17 species of butterfly that nectar from it. It's non-native, but don't be put off: when it comes to nectar borders, we've found that a mix of natives and non-natives can be an effective way to maximize the amount of nectar on offer throughout the year.

If your nectar border will not receive a lot of sun, look out for species such as nettle-leaved bellflower, columbine, and hellebore, which all grow well in shade and provide plenty of nectar. Then there's red campion, which thrives in shade and spreads well, and is a favourite for spring-emerging insects including the brimstone butterfly.

The best time to plant a border is in spring or autumn. If the plot will be accessible from all sides, position taller species in the middle; if it backs on to a boundary (such as a fence, hedge, or building), place taller plants against that boundary. Then continue planting outwards in ever-decreasing heights towards the front of the border. Aim to completely fill the area – the more dense the planting, the less maintenance required later, as the ground cover will help to retain moisture and discourage weed growth. Once your border is completely planted, water the plants well to help them settle in.

WHO LIVES THERE

As well as attracting all kinds of pollinators, bees – especially bumblebees and honeybees – will thrive on the nectar your borders provide. Try planting pulmonaria, which is a favourite for many bee species, or hellebore plants

YOU COULD PLANT ...

COLUMBINE

CONEFLOWER

FOXGLOVE

HELLEBORE

LAVENDER

MARJORAM

NEPETA

NETTLE-LEAVED BELLFLOWER

RED CAMPION

SNEEZEWORT

VERBENA BONARIENSIS

VIPERS BUGLOSS

A Sneezewort **B** Coneflower
C Verbena bonariensis **D** Common fleabane

A

B

(particularly stinking hellebore) to attract early bumblebees from around February onwards.

A well-packed nectar border can also support many varieties of slugs and snails, which in turn provide great food for any passing hedgehogs or song thrushes. Moths visiting the border at night will also be a welcome snack for any bats in the area.

LOOKING AFTER YOUR BORDERS

As the nectar border begins to grow, look out for any weeds that might compete for nutrients and space with your plants. After a while you should find that this becomes less of an issue, as the plants grow and the amount of bare ground decreases.

A Peacock butterfly **B** Bumblebee **C** Hoverfly
D Meadow brown butterfly

Other than this occasional weeding, managing your border is fairly straightforward. Leave old growth over the winter, then cut it back in early spring in preparation for the new growing season. We prefer this approach to cutting back plants in the autumn, as this removes potential cover and food for wildlife. With our approach, invertebrates can use the old growth to hibernate in, while birds can feed on the old seedheads.

Woodier species, such as lavender, should be trimmed back after they have flowered. Many plants, such as nepeta and geranium, will flower again and again if you trim them back after their initial flowering, while deadheading the old flowers of buddlejas will ensure the plant continues to flower for many more weeks, providing nectar for late-summer-emerging butterflies.

As your border matures, you may occasionally need to dig up and divide or replace older, larger plants. Keep an eye out too for biennials such as viper's bugloss, in case they don't re-establish themselves from dispersed seed.

Attract rare butterflies and
moths by creating your own
slice of the beautiful downland
habitat that they rely on.

A LIMESTONE BANK

Wildflowers just love alkaline soils. Rich in limestone or chalk, these soils are typically free-draining and offer only a limited amount of nutrients, which discourages persistent, broad-leaved weeds and vigorous grass growth. As a result, wildflowers and fine grasses have the perfect opportunity to flourish, attracting a whole host of other wildlife in the process, including rare butterflies and moths, common lizards, and slow worms.

A limestone or chalk bank replicates the kind of habitat you might find across downland or in an abandoned quarry. It may seem like an unusual feature in your plot, but as you are reading this book, it's probably fair to say that you have an open mind when it comes to wilding your garden. Think of this project as an alternative to a traditional border: a flower-rich area of your garden, only with wildflowers rather than a mix of native and non-native herbaceous perennials.

This project replicates wild downland, where as many as 20 wildflower and grass species can be found in a single square metre (11 sq ft).

Cover your mound of soil and rubble with a weed-control membrane, then secure it in place with large stones until you're ready to add the aggregate.

We prefer to use a crushed aggregate such as limestone or chalk. Make sure the material has small enough pieces to plant into easily.

This photo, taken three months after we created the bank, shows how the wildflowers and grasses have established themselves within the aggregate.

HOW TO MAKE IT

Using your garden's aspect (see pages 14–15), find a sunny position for your bank. Ideally, it should run from east to west to ensure that one side will be south-facing. If you can't make this work in your garden, don't worry. Choose the brightest spot you can, and if necessary, seek out shade-loving species that can grow in chalky soils; we would recommend nettle-leaved bellflower and wild strawberry plants.

The bigger the bank can be, the better; we would recommend something around 3m (9ft) long, 1m (3ft) high, and 2m (6ft) wide in a typical suburban garden.

Unless you have large quantities of limestone and chalk already to hand, the most sensible and cost-effective way to build your bank is with soil dug up from other projects, such as a natural pond (see pages 62–71). If you have any rubble left over on your plot from recent building work, you could mix this into the soil, too. The nutrient quality of the bank itself is unimportant, as your wildflowers and grasses will not be directly planted into this medium.

> If you have a large mound of soil left over from digging a pond, this is a great way to repurpose it.

Pile your soil mix into place to create the bank, then cover the entire surface with a weed-control membrane to give your wildflowers and grasses the best chance at settling in. Secure the membrane in place with any large stones or rocks you have to hand.

Now it's time for your chosen aggregate – chalk or limestone, whichever you're able to source in your area. You could buy 20mm (¹³⁄₁₆in) limestone in tonne bags from builder's merchants, but the stones will look very uniform – and not at all natural. We've found that a mixture of rough stones of varying size, with dust mixed in, works best. We suggest a phone call and visit to a local quarry to explain your needs.

Using a wheelbarrow, tip your aggregate onto the bank to create a 15cm- (6in-) thick layer on top of the membrane. This will allow the plants to really get their roots down into the aggregate and grow strongly, which in turn will help them cope better in drought conditions (which can be a risk with south-facing plants). Once the bank is completely covered, carefully walk all over the area to tread the aggregate into place.

At this stage, you might want to consider adding a few larger pieces of stone here and there. As well as adding some variety and visual interest to the bank, if you group a few well-placed rocks together in various places, you can create areas of refuge and hibernation sites for reptiles and amphibians.

YOU COULD PLANT...

BIRD'S-FOOT TREFOIL

COMMON TOADFLAX

CRESTED DOG'S-TAIL

DARK MULLEIN

FIELD SCABIOUS

GREATER KNAPWEED

HORSESHOE VETCH

KIDNEY VETCH

MARJORAM

QUAKING GRASS

ROCK ROSE

SHEEP'S FESCUE

SLENDER CREEPING RED FESCUE

VIPERS BUGLOSS

WHAT TO PLANT

As this project is designed to quickly replicate a piece of downland in your garden, you'll need to plant a diverse selection of species to mimic the habitat that wildlife would expect to find in the wild. Use the Plant List on pages 182–86 to find a range of suitable wildflowers and wild grasses.

Of all the plants you could choose from, we would particularly recommend marjoram: by the height of summer, it will attract an abundance of insects thanks to the nectar it provides. Viper's bugloss is another excellent choice. Few plants are quite as loved by bees as this purple–blue flower, while small and Essex skipper butterflies will also flock to its nectar. Finally, no chalk or limestone bank would be complete without a few vetches. Whether bird's-foot trefoil, horseshoe vetch, or kidney vetch, all three will attract a huge array of insects.

A Horseshoe vetch B Viper's bugloss
C Marjoram D Rock rose

A Wool carder bee **B** Holly blue butterfly
C Brimstone butterfly **D** Slow worm

The best times to plant your wildflowers are during spring or autumn. We prefer to use 9cm (3½in) potted plants for this project, as they establish faster and are more likely to thrive during the first few months than plug plants, which can easily dry out in well-drained limestone. We would not recommend sowing wildflower seed for this project, as many soil-specific wildflowers can be tricky to grow from seed. At least with a potted plant, you don't need to worry about it germinating!

For the wild grasses, on the other hand, we have had success with both sowing seed or planting 9cm (3½in) potted plants, although you may find that potted grasses are less readily available. Whichever option you choose, sow or plant your grasses in September or October, after you have planted your wildflowers. If you opt to use seed, the grasses should begin to sprout around 4–6 weeks after sowing.

WHO LIVES THERE

Due to the hot, often sun-baked nature of these micro-habitats, you can expect to find a different group of creatures calling this home than you

YOU COULD HELP...

would in a herbaceous border. The female small blue butterfly, for example, can sense the larval food plant of kidney vetch up to 10km (6 miles) away. Mining bees also love these well-drained banks, while the warmth of the habitat means that you're likely to spot common lizards, slow worms, and other cold-blooded reptiles warming themselves with the sun's rays.

LOOKING AFTER YOUR BANK

Once your bank is planted and settling in, you can sit back, relax, and admire the results of your hard work. The bank itself shouldn't need much maintenance, just a cut-back with a pair of shears once a year in the spring. Cut back when the birds have eaten the last seeds and the insects have finished using your bank for cover and hibernation through the winter.

WILDFLOWER MEADOWS

Forget sterile, perfectly manicured lawns. By creating your own mini-meadow, glade, or flowering lawn, you'll be able to support a huge variety of pollinating insects and other forms of wildlife.

INTRODUCTION

It's hard to imagine a meadow without hearing the beautiful song of skylarks or the gentle buzzing of grasshoppers and crickets. Meadow brown and marbled white butterflies lift up from the long grasses, with swallows chasing and feeding on the thousands of meadow insects.

Losing even a single square metre of such a meadow is heartbreaking, but the truth is that meadows are disappearing on a massive scale: in Great Britain, for example, more than 97 per cent of wildflower meadows have been lost since the 1930s – that's 3 million hectares (7.5 million acres). We can only begin to comprehend the effect this has had on wildlife.

For many of us, a colourful meadow means vivid red poppies, sunshine-yellow corn marigolds, and sky-blue cornflowers buzzing with bees. These plants used to be common as agricultural "weeds", scattered across the fertile soils of wheat and barley fields, and are now known as the plants that make up a cornfield annual meadow. As farming techniques changed, we began to lose these vibrant countryside blooms; now we see splashes of colours only where the farming methods have allowed the plants to grow.

The biodiversity of a meadow can be staggering – it can contain up to 40 species per square metre.

The nostalgia of a "hay meadow" brings to mind visions of running through long grasses with ox-eye daisies. These perennial wildflower meadows ("perennial" means they'll come up every year and, with the correct management, will become more spectacular with each passing year) are extraordinary, both ecologically and aesthetically. They require minimal management – only one cut a year towards the end of summer. Unlike cornfield annual meadows, perennial wildflower meadows grow best on poor soil.

You may be surprised to find out that you might already have a type of meadow in your own back garden. If you have a lawn that hasn't been fertilized or had weedkiller applied for many years, and it has been mown and the cuttings removed, it's safe to say you have a wildflower meadow simply desperate to grow and flower. Lawns are a hugely neglected habitat, with masses of potential for turning back into meadow, with little effort.

Whichever of these flower-rich habitats you want to create at home, we'll show you how – let's help put these wildlife havens back on the map.

Spectacular wildflower
meadows can thrive in even
the smallest of gardens –
especially those with poor soil.

A PERENNIAL WILDFLOWER MEADOW

One of the sayings we hear so often from people with small or average sized gardens is "I would love to have a proper meadow but I haven't got the room". This statement couldn't be further from the truth. We have worked in countless gardens over the years, and every one has had the potential for at least a couple of square metres of wildflower meadow.

The misconception that a meadow has to be large is a common one, and understandable when we think that many wild meadows are indeed sizeable. But it is much better to have 10sq m (108sq ft) of diverse meadow habitat in a garden context than 10 hectares (25 acres) of grassland, consisting of just a few species of non-native rye grass that hardly support any wildlife. We have seen garden meadows that have become so botanically and ecologically rich, they'd make any nature reserve warden jump for joy.

Simple mown paths guide your route around this large wildflower meadow, featuring greater knapweed and field scabious.

PLANNING YOUR MEADOW

First, consider the garden's aspect (see pages 14–15). It is best to choose a sunny and fairly well-draining area, as large as space allows.

Wildflower meadows work best on soils that are poor, starved of the nutrients that would, in fertile soils, allow coarse grasses and perennial weed species (such as broad-leaved dock and creeping thistle) to thrive. Many meadows have failed over the years, despite people's best efforts, simply because there was too much goodness in the soil from the start. Even if you have a lush, colourful meadow for the first year or so, the meadow will quickly decline and revert to weeds and coarse grasses.

If you live on limestone or chalk, or perhaps well-draining sandy soils, you are in a lucky position of not having to worry about excessive nutrients. If, however, you are one of the vast majority of garden owners who are faced with fairly fertile topsoil, you will need to need to dig down to your garden's subsoil before you can sow your meadow.

> So often we hear from people saying they'd love a proper meadow but don't have the room.

Reaching this low-nutrient layer beneath your garden's richer, darker topsoil takes some effort, but in time you'll be rewarded with a well-established meadow.

There are two main ways you can reach the subsoil, either of which should ideally take place around June or July. One option is to simply strip the topsoil off. If the area is small, digging by hand should be fine, but for areas larger than a few square metres, you will want to hire a contractor with a mini-digger. You will probably need to dig down to a depth of about 15–25cm (6–10in) to reach the subsoil; it is usually obvious as you dig because the soil colour becomes lighter and often the texture changes, too. The topsoil that you remove can be used to create a vegetable-growing patch or to enrich an area you plan to plant with trees and shrubs (see pages 28–59).

Wildflower seed is more likely to germinate successfully when the soil is fine. By running a rotovator across the area you wish to sow (ideally when the ground is dry), you'll give the soil a fine, crumbly texture.

Sowing wildflower seed can produce stunning results. This image was taken a little under two years after seed was sown; since then, the plot has transformed into a lush and vibrant mini-meadow.

If it is not practical to lower your soil level by removing all of the topsoil, there is a second option. First, dig the topsoil off the proposed area and place it to one side. Next, dig out a large layer of subsoil, and keep this in a separate pile. Tip the topsoil back into the bottom of this hole and even it out, then top it off with the subsoil. This option is slightly more complicated but will keep the ground level unchanged.

Whichever method you use, once your subsoil is ready, prepare the seed bed by digging and turning the soil (or by rotovating) and raking the surface free of stones and debris. As this soil is nutrient-poor, it is unlikely that there will be much weed growth here; that said, it is best to wait four to six weeks before sowing seed to allow any potential weeds to start growing. If any weeds do grow, simply dig or rotovate again to remove them.

YOU COULD SOW...

AGRIMONY

BIRD'S-FOOT TREFOIL

BLADDER CAMPION

COMMON KNAPWEED

COMMON SORREL

COWSLIP

FIELD SCABIOUS

LADY'S BEDSTRAW

MARJORAM

OX-EYE DAISY

RED CLOVER

YARROW

WHAT TO SOW

We recommend your seed mix should comprise around 80 per cent wild grass species and 20 per cent wildflowers. There are many excellent seed merchants who are happy to advise you and can even create custom seed mixtures.

Although you would want to primarily sow perennial species, feel free to include annuals and biennials, too; in fact, we would encourage you to do so. As well as providing pollinators with more nectar variety, by sowing a mix of different seed types, you will create a longer flowering period. You could, for instance, add some cornfield annuals to your seed mix (see page 129). These wildflowers will bloom through the first summer, acting as a

A Ox-eye daisy   B Common knapweed
C Field scabious   D Primrose

nurse crop for the small, developing perennial wildflowers and grasses growing beneath. The annuals will only last for one season, but will provide a spectacular display while you wait for the meadow to properly start to flower in year two. At this stage, any biennials you might have sown (such as wild carrot, teasel, and viper's bugloss, and ox-eye daisies) will appear along with your perennials, providing a fantastic display of flowers as the second summer progresses.

Be sure to include some yellow rattle in your initial mixture, too. This brilliant parasitic annual takes nutrients from the roots of other plants, mainly grasses, which reduces their vigour and, in turn, allows its neighbouring wildflowers to thrive.

You can continue to resow biennial seed every other autumn if you wish. Do not resow annual seed, however, as they will have trouble competing with the perennials once they are fully established.

HOW TO SOW

The best time to sow a meadow is from mid-September to the end of October. Choose a mild day for sowing; you don't want rain or too much wind, as this can cause problems, particularly with fine seeds or on clay sites.

Calculate the amount of seed you'll need to cover your area by multiplying the length of the area by the width to give the square meterage. Then multiply the square meterage by the sowing rate of 4 grams per sq m (11sq ft). You can either mix the seed with sand in a bucket and sow by hand, or use a seed broadcaster. Divide the seed mixture in two. Sow one half of the seed in one direction across the site, and the second half perpendicular (90 degrees) to that. This method ensures a healthy distribution of seed. Once your seed is sown, you can roll it in with a hand roller, tread the soil down with your feet (preferably with someone to help on larger sites!), or gently rake the seed to achieve good seed-to-soil contact.

Keep people and animals off the newly sown meadow. Seedlings should begin to appear after four to six weeks. First, you'll notice a fine green covering of grass, which tends to germinate faster than the wildflowers. By spring, the meadow will be growing strongly, ready for mowing (see opposite).

WHO LIVES THERE

As well as the beautiful array of wildflowers in your meadow, you can marvel at all the wonderful wildlife that this new habitat will attract. Look for mining bees nesting in bare patches of soil and common shrews foraging through the grass. Admire beautiful gatekeeper and ringlet butterflies as they weave their way through the fine grasses, and the colourful day flying six-spot burnet moths supping the nectar on knapweed and devil's bit scabious.

LOOKING AFTER A PERENNIAL MEADOW

During its first full summer, mow the meadow regularly on a high setting and collect the cuttings. This will discourage any annual weeds, strengthen the developing wildflowers and grasses, and prevent the nutrients in the cuttings from enriching the soil.

By the end of the first summer, the plants should have developed a good coverage, and be around 60cm (24in) tall. At this point, the meadow will be ready for its first "hay cut". This can take place from early August onwards; if you still have abundant nectar-rich flowers, you could delay cutting for a few weeks to give any remaining insects the chance to complete their life cycles and enjoy the last available nectar from the flowers.

> By the end of the first summer, the meadow should have a good coverage of wildflowers.

The most environmentally and ecologically friendly method of cutting the meadow is with garden shears (or with a scythe if you've had training) to avoid any harm to wildlife. Any small mammals, invertebrates, amphibians, and reptiles can disperse as you slowly and quietly approach. Using a petrol strimmer to cut the meadow may be an efficient way but can cause serious harm to wildlife, even in experienced hands. For this reason, we recommend using them only as a last resort, and users should take extreme care and precautions when operating them.

A Common blue butterfly **B** Holly blue butterfly
C Common lizard

When you have cut your meadow, leave the cuttings for a few days to give them time to dry and drop their seeds, then rake off and put the cuttings to good use – pile them up to form habitat heaps in quiet places around the meadow (see also pages 152–55), spread under trees and hedges as a mulch, or slowly use bit by bit in an active compost bin.

Inspect your meadow area. If you notice any particularly grassy areas developing at this stage, oversow with fresh yellow rattle seed in October to open the sward (grassy top layer) structure in the meadow and allow wildflowers more room to seed and grow next year. You may need to repeat this stage for the first few years, but in time you should find that yellow rattle does well on its own, and won't need regular resowing.

The following year, leave the meadow to grow undisturbed until the annual hay cut. This can happen as early as August, although we would recommend September. Before too long, the biennial seeds you sowed

C

YOU COULD HELP...

during the first year will emerge. If you have managed the meadow correctly, you shouldn't need to resow any seed aside from yellow rattle, but if coverage becomes patchy over time, simply resow as needed during the autumn months. By following this simple "one cut a year" management process, you will maintain excellent floral diversity, and, in turn, support a greater array of plant and animal species in your wildflower meadow habitat.

If you have always dreamed of having your own meadow, there is no better time to start planning it than now. It doesn't matter if you are in the middle of a crowded urban street, or amid vast agricultural swathes of monocultural crops in rural countryside, your little meadow will probably be the best for miles around.

Summoning up images of a romantic countryside, nectar-rich cornfield annuals are the stars of the show throughout June and July.

A CORNFIELD ANNUAL MEADOW

Some of us still remember the sight of vast swathes of wheat fields coloured by the red, blue, and yellow of poppies, cornflowers, and corn marigold. These fields provided valuable nectar for pollinators up and down the country. Unfortunately, it is hard nowadays for any of these wonderful wildflowers to survive in arable areas, due to increasingly intensive farming methods used in agriculture today.

You can counter this decline by creating your own cornfield annual meadow. The simplest way to create a colourful, nectar-rich meadow in a short space of time is by sowing a patch of cornfield annuals. These plants establish and grow very quickly, and in the course of their short life provide plenty of nectar for insects and seeds for birds.

A diverse range of colours make up the bucolic image of a cornfield annual meadow in summer.

Cornfield annual meadows are ideal if you have a troublesome patch of ground that receives a good amount of sunlight. Whether you're faced with poor clay soil where herbaceous perennials struggle to grow or rich fertile loam where a perennial wildflower meadow is out of the question due to excessive soil fertility, cornfield annuals are the perfect solution.

WHAT TO SOW

Over many generations, cornfield annuals have adapted to not merely persist but thrive in "disturbed" settings: the annual ploughing of a field provides the perfect environment for these annual wildflowers to thrive. Wildflower seeds can remain in the ground for years and only germinate when disturbed; the seeds of the common poppy, for instance, can germinate decades after dropping onto the ground. As well as the poppy, the most characteristic species of wildflowers in a cornfield annual meadow include the word "corn" in their names – think, corn chamomile, corncockle, cornflower, and corn marigold. Corn chamomile will bring the classic daisy feel to your meadow, looking similar to an ox-eye daisy, and will grow best on sandy and well-drained soils. The corncockle's beautiful pink flower has suffered massive declines in the countryside, and is worth sowing for this reason alone. The deep-blue flowers of the cornflower are breathtaking when sown in numbers, and its flowers prove irresistible to pollinators and humans alike. Then there is the sunshine-yellow corn marigold, a must for any cornfield meadow, which is easily grown and provides welcome nectar for passing insects.

YOU COULD SOW...

COMMON POPPY

CORN CHAMOMILE

CORNFLOWER

CORNCOCKLE

CORN MARIGOLD

PREPARING THE MEADOW

These annual wildflowers are undemanding, so it is easy to find a suitable space for them in your garden. When it comes to choosing a location for your meadow, the only considerations are finding ground that isn't

A Corncockle B Common poppy
C Cornflower D Corn marigold

permanently waterlogged, receives a good deal of sunlight, and is preferably away from mature trees.

When you have decided on the best place for your meadow, prepare the soil in August, well in advance of seeding, by removing any persistent weed species, fallen leaves, and large stones, and turning the soil over using a spade or a rotovator. Once you have a good tilth (a fine bed of soil), rake it level and leave the area for four to six weeks. Within that time, the widespread germination of weed seedlings will appear. Once the area looks green with young weed growth, turn the soil over and rake level again, and you should have a weed-free seedbed ready for sowing.

SOWING THE SEEDS

The best time of the year to sow cornfield annuals is between the middle of September and the end of October. This timing will ensure a good germination of seeds by the end of the year, and the young plants will then grow strongly the following spring. If you have missed the chance to sow in autumn, you can still sow the seed in April. But a dry spring can create difficult conditions for germination, and seedlings can really struggle through May and June without any serious rainfall, so be sure to water your plants well during dry spells.

The best sowing rates for cornfield annuals are 2–3 grams of seed per sq m (11sq ft), but in the first year it's probably best to allow up to 4 grams per sq m (11sq ft) to ensure a good coverage.

> For larger areas, we mix our seed into a bucket of sand so we can see where we've already sown.

You can scatter the seed by hand, which is easy enough on small areas of just a few square metres. On large-scale meadows, though, we find it is best to mix the seed in a bucket of sand, which bulks it up to make the seed go further, and highlights exactly where the seed has fallen. You can also use a seed broadcaster to ensure an even distribution of seed.

As this front garden was looking quite tired and weedy, we took the opportunity to transform it into a mini wildflower meadow.

Once the area was cleared, we used a rotovator to turn over the soil, and remove any weeds and stones to produce a fine bed of soil (known as a tilth).

As this meadow was quite small, we scattered the seed by hand, first by walking up and down the length of the plot, and then across the width.

Once sown, the meadow was in full bloom by the following summer, adding an eye-catching splash of colour in front of the house.

A Red-tailed bumblebee **B** Hoverflies
C Six-spot burnet moth

Whichever method of sowing you choose, we recommend dividing the seed in half. Walk across the whole area, sowing one half in one direction and the remaining half perpendicular (90 degrees) to it.

After sowing the seed, either tread the surface down by walking back and forth across the soil, use a hand roller, or lightly rake the area to gently cover the seed with soil, guaranteeing good seed-to-soil contact.

WHO LIVES THERE

Prepare yourself for a spectacular performance in the summer months as the wildflowers put on a colourful show. Enjoy the many different species of bumblebee foraging for nectar among the scarlet-red poppies and sky-blue cornflowers. Observe busy honeybees as they hop from flower to flower, laden with golden pollen, and watch butterflies such as the common blue sipping nectar from corncockles.

BUFF-TAILED BUMBLEBEE

COMMON CARDER BEE

GARDEN BUMBLEBEE

HONEYBEE

HOVER FLY

RED-TAILED BUMBLEBEE

THICK-LEGGED FLOWER BEETLE

TREE BUMBLEBEE

WHITE-TAILED BUMBLEBEE

LOOKING AFTER THE MEADOW

After autumn germination and slow winter growth, there'll be a nice coverage of green by April or May, followed by strong spring growth and flowers in the summer. After a good show of flowers, the plants will go to seed (mid-July onwards).

Once most of the seed has dropped, cut the area down. We recommend using garden shears to avoid any harm to wildlife. Rake the vegetation off; you can use this to create habitat heaps (see pages 152–55) or to mulch the base of trees and hedges. When the area is cleared, dig over or rotovate the soil in preparation for sowing the new generation of wildflowers. As this is an annual meadow, you'll need to resow it each year; we've had great success with night-scented stock, poached-egg plant, and black-eyed Susan.

Let's change the way we look at
our lawns and transform what is
a fairly sterile patch of grass into
a brilliant wildlife haven.

A FLOWERING LAWN

There are billions of lawns across the globe. That's an awful lot of grass and a lot of mowing. For a wildlife gardener, a lawn has massive potential – a large and often sunny area that's crying out for some tweaking to make it welcoming to wildlife. And for those situations where a meadow is too much work or not allowed (in some rental properties, for instance), a flowering lawn is a fantastic asset for attracting wildlife.

Mowing the lawn has for decades been an obsession for many homeowners. From village greens to inner-city parks, grass is treated the same – it's mown short. This process prevents any existing wildflowers from flowering and reduces the likelihood of any small insects surviving.

The basic principle of creating a flowering lawn is to introduce wildflowers into an existing lawn, and manage the mowing regime so that a mini-meadow can flourish. This project may take a year to establish, but from early on, you will see a huge increase in the number of insects visiting your garden.

This flowering lawn, which has been left
to grow over the summer, offers a vivid
display of poppies and corn chamomile.

Before we start planting, we always place the plants roughly where we will want them to go; in this case, around 30–60cm (1–2ft) apart. This helps ensure an even distribution, and gives us an idea of the finished outcome.

Having being allowed to grow long for the first time, this lawn soon burst into flower. This bee orchid, for instance, had been waiting for its opportunity to bloom.

CREATING A FLOWERING LAWN

The best times of year to tackle such a project are early spring and autumn. April or October would be ideal, when there's enough warmth and moisture in the soil to enable plants to establish quickly.

First, cut the lawn on your mower's lowest setting. This may seem counterintuitive, but now you need to start seeing this area as a meadow, not an immaculate but sterile carpet of grass. Cutting the lawn back hard creates bare gaps of soil where new plants can be planted. After mowing, remove the cuttings and compost them or use as mulch.

Then, grab a good garden rake (a metal spring or leaf rake is best) and rake the area vigorously. This process removes any missed grass cuttings and accumulated thatch and moss, and will open up many spaces for planting. Again, use this raked material as a mulch or add to a habitat heap (see pages 152–55). Now you're ready to plant.

WHAT TO PLANT

Up close, an existing lawn is likely to have quite a few species of so-called "weeds". These weeds are, in fact, beautiful wildflowers, such as cat's ears, red clover, self-heal, and lesser celandine, that have adapted to creep along the ground (to escape the mower blades) and may never have had a chance to flower.

In addition to these resident wildflowers you'll want to plant a selection of new species to really bring your lawn to life (see pages 182–86). As a general rule, you don't need to plant more than 10 plants per sq m (11 sq ft). Choose a good selection

> Use bigger potted plants, as they're much more likely to survive competition from the nearby grasses.

with as many different species as you can, which will not only guarantee a good variety of flowers and nectar through the season, but will also mean that there'll always be some plants that manage to thrive. We'd recommend planting 10 species – then, say, at least six should thrive. If you only planted lots of one variety and very few took, they could all slowly disappear.

Be sure to check flowering times and growth habits so that you can decide how many you'll need and how best to arrange them. For example, a single knapweed plant will grow into a fairly tall and wide clump, whereas smaller cowslips work well in groups as they flower in spring when there is much less vegetation around.

While many people recommend the use of cheaper plug plants when planting into existing lawns, we've had much more success with 9cm (3½in) potted plants and find it's often more cost-effective, too. A larger, well-rooted wildflower in a pot is likely to survive in this situation, whereas small plants are more likely to fail as they compete with the vigorous surrounding grasses.

Once you're happy with the plants' arrangement on the lawn, use a good trowel or a planting spade to dig a hole deep enough to accommodate the plant's roots comfortably. Remove the plant from its pot and gently tease out some of the roots – for a healthier plant in a shorter timeframe. Use your hands to back fill around the plant with the soil, firming it down around the roots as you go. There is no need for any additional compost or fertilizer – these are native wildflowers and can thrive in tougher conditions.

Once you have all the plants in the ground, sprinkle perennial wildflower seed mix over the top to encourage a few finer native grass species and fill in any gaps. Finally, water the area well, even if it is

YOU COULD PLANT...

BIRD'S-FOOT TREFOIL

COWSLIP

DANDELION

LADY'S BEDSTRAW

MEADOW BUTTERCUP

DAISY

PRIMROSE

RED CLOVER

SAINFOIN

SELF-HEAL

SORREL

YARROW

A Cowslip **B** Ox-eye daisy
C Red clover **D** Bird's-foot trefoil

A Brown argus butterfly **B** Garden snail
C Blackbird **D** Mint moth

a damp day or the ground seems damp enough. Watering ensures the soil settles around the roots and gives the seeds a good head start in the germination process.

WHO LIVES THERE

Aside from the obvious creatures that will frequent your flowering lawn, such as butterflies and bees, these plants will provide shelter for other insects such as woodlice and spiders, as well as moth and butterfly larvae.

LOOKING AFTER A FLOWERING LAWN

If you plant wildflowers in the spring, leave the area for at least a month before you mow it on a high setting. If there still isn't a huge amount of growth on the newly planted wildflowers, mow around them to keep the spring grass in check. As soon as the plants are growing well, begin gently

C

D

YOU COULD HELP...

BROWN ARGUS BUTTERFLY

CENTIPEDE

GARDEN SNAIL

GARDEN SPIDER

HEDGEHOG

MINT MOTH

WOODLICE

mowing over the top of them. Continue mowing the lawn regularly, always on a high setting and be sure to remove the cuttings. You may have only a few flowers in the first summer as the plants are putting their energy into rooting rather than flowering. If you plant in October, you won't need to do much initially – leave the area to settle over winter. Come spring, once the grass begins to grow, mow it regularly, say every two to four weeks.

After this, the most critical thing to do each year is to keep the grass in check through March, April, and May. By June, the area can probably be left to flower for six to eight weeks through the summer. The beauty of this project is that you can change the mowing regime to suit yourself and the flowers.

You don't need to own a piece of ancient woodland to create your own shady dell and little patch of wildlife heaven.

A WOODLAND GLADE

Many gardens are blessed with established mature trees, which are a wonderful habitat in their own right. Dappled or heavy shade, coupled with dry conditions, can make gardening under trees quite difficult and, in some cases, it can seem impossible to make anything grow there. But, as with so many other examples in wildlife gardening, nature holds the answers you need.

Think of a woodland glade and no doubt that image will feature foxgloves, primroses, and bluebells as far as the eye can see. These colourful plants are completely happy growing in the shade of the tree canopy, without any additional care. Many species of plants, particularly native wildflowers, positively thrive in these habitats, so by replicating this in a garden setting where conventional planting simply wouldn't work, we can create shady, nectar-rich glades that offer a wonderful fuelling station for invertebrates.

The red campion growing at the edge of this woodland glade is the perfect spot for speckled wood butterflies.

WHAT TO PLANT

This project is best seen as a "drift of flowers" that sweeps under some trees. You can plant underneath a single silver birch or an entire copse if you wish, but do choose a broad variety of plant species to ensure at least some of them will succeed and to make sure you have flowers throughout the seasons, too. Very soon you'll be hearing the gentle buzz of bees visiting foxglove bells and can delight at a carpet of violets and bluebells.

CREATING A WOODLAND GLADE

It is best to carry out this project in early spring, after the leaf fall of autumn, and well before the greening of the canopy. Spring is also a good time of year to establish plants, as the ground is getting warmer and the intense dryness of summer hasn't yet set in.

First, clear the ground of unwanted vegetation and leaf cover. This waste can easily be added to habitat heaps (see pages 152–55) or piled up for cover for hedgehogs, and leaves also make great mulch around other trees and shrubs.

Once cleared, if you wish to dig over the area to make planting easier, do so, but be mindful of any large tree roots nearby. If you're lucky, you may find that years of leaf litter build-up means you don't need to dig over the whole area as it will already be quite workable. More often than not, however, the ground beneath trees is exceptionally dry and quite hard. If this is the case, then it may be easier to dig only the holes for the plants as you plant them.

Look at the Plant List on pages 182–86 and select a mixture of species. We like to use 9cm (3½in) potted wildflowers, rather

YOU COULD PLANT...

BETONY

BLUEBELL

DOG VIOLET

FOXGLOVE

GARLIC MUSTARD

LESSER CELANDINE

PRIMROSE

RED CAMPION

SNOWDROP

STINKING HELLEBORE

SWEET WOODRUFF

WILD GARLIC

A Snake's-head fritillary B Foxglove
C Garlic mustard D Primrose

A Speckled wood butterfly **B** Lesser stag beetle
C Robin **D** Common lizard

than plug plants, as they establish rapidly in their first season, so you can expect quite a few flowers in the first spring and summer. But it will be the second year onwards that you will have a great display of wildflowers once the plants have matured. Group together the same species where possible. Insects love finding tighter groups of the same nectar source; and a large clump of red campion, for example, looks better than individual plants here and there. Space out the pots and, once you're happy with the arrangement, plant each one following the instructions on page 138 and water them in well.

If you want a meadow-like glade, sow a woodland grass mix between the flowers, and mow the whole area, including the flowers, on a high setting once the grasses and wildflowers are established (see pages 122–23). This helps the grasses to thrive, and provides a habitat for butterflies, including the speckled wood, which lay their eggs on grasses such as cock's-foot and false brome.

C

D

YOU COULD HELP...

BLACKBIRD
BRIMSTONE BUTTERFLY
CHIFFCHAFF
COMMON LIZARD
GREAT SPOTTED WOODPECKER
SLOW WORM
SPECKLED WOOD BUTTERFLY
TAWNY OWL
WOOD MOUSE

WHO LIVES THERE

This "edge of woodland" habitat will encourage a huge amount of wildlife. The nectar that these specialized wildflowers provide will help spring emerging insects such as the early bumblebee and the first emerging male brimstone butterflies, which will make the most of primrose flowers.

LOOKING AFTER A GLADE

The management of a woodland glade is easy – simply cut it in late summer (see page 123), rake off the area, before the leaves fall, and add that vegetation to a habitat heap (see pages 152–55). That's it until next spring – if there are any empty patches or plants that have failed, you can simply plant more plants in these spots or sow with a woodland-edge seed mix.

WELCOME MORE WILDLIFE

Complete your wild garden with a few
added touches, including refuges for
birds, bees, and reptiles – along with
some tips and tricks to give an extra
boost to local wildlife.

INTRODUCTION

It's been our pleasure to visit some truly magnificent wildlife gardens over the years – pieces of land where the owners have worked tirelessly for years, sometimes decades, to do everything they possibly can to encourage and help wildlife. They have created meadows, constructed ponds, swapped patios for flowering lawns, and even planted woodlands. These remarkable gardens are so rich in wildlife, you can quickly forget that you are in a garden at all! But even when we visit spaces like these, we soon point out to these same people just how many additional features they could add to further improve the garden's potential to support local wildlife.

One of the most wonderful aspects of creating a wild garden is the level of detail you can go to when catering for all the species you can reasonably expect to attract to your plot. It is simply brilliant to watch the first newts explore your new wildlife pond, to hear the first hedgehog snuffling through your mini-meadow, and to glimpse the first common pipistrelle bats hunting over your native hedgerow.

But once the newts have bred and left the pond, where will they hunt and hibernate? Is there somewhere safe for hedgehogs to breed and then

A pond and plants can
bring lots of wildlife to
your plot, but don't forget
the other projects you can
do to encourage creatures
into your garden.

spend the winter? Can birds reach feeders in safety? How many ancient trees with holes in can the bats find in your neighbourhood or will they need boxes erecting?

After you've covered all the major habitats – woodland, wildlife pond, nectar border, and meadow – there is still much more you can do to create places for many key species to use regularly, or even take up residence in. In this chapter, we look at the additional "extras" that make a wildlife garden special, with something to suit every ability and garden size, including simple log piles, specially designed bat and bird boxes, and a compost bin that doubles as a sanctuary for cold-blooded reptiles.

Don't feel like you have to squeeze every single project into your garden. If you haven't the time to build a bird box, consider buying one instead. If you can't build a dry stone wall, a stone pile or habitat heap will still be a great addition to your plot. This chapter isn't about completing a checklist. Instead, it's about asking yourself if there is anything else you can realistically do to support wildlife; the finishing touches that make your garden as wild as it can be.

Don't view pieces of stone, grass cuttings, branches, or leaves as garden waste – they can all provide valuable habitats in your plot.

HABITAT HEAPS

Nothing goes to waste in a wildlife garden. If you think that grass cuttings from a flowering lawn, cut branches from a native hedgerow or shrub, or stones found while gardening or excavating for a pond are waste, think again. All of this "waste" can be used to create habitats, solving disposal issues and benefiting wildlife at the same time (see also pages 156–59). Taking on just one of the following projects will expand the numbers and variety of species of animals that visit and live in your garden.

A BRASH PILE

One of the most basic heaps you can create is what we refer to as a "brash pile" – basically a rough pile of cut branches, woody plant stems, and hay or cut vegetation. These piles are best situated on the edge of a meadow or coppice belt or under a native hedge.

Use the larger branches to form the bottom of the pile and top with the smaller branches and other vegetation. It's as simple as that, and by

A common lizard basking in the early morning sun on the top of a log pile.

creating this habitat you will be providing an excellent hibernation site for hedgehogs, nesting opportunities for birds (especially in larger heaps), and a refuge for small mammals, too. Top the pile up each autumn with meadow cuttings and prunings from shrubs. Creating piles in this way is so much better than having a bonfire or incinerating garden waste.

A COVERED HEAP

Take the brash pile a step further to create a covered heap that's a great habitat for grass snakes. Choose a quiet corner of the garden for this project, where there is minimal disturbance, some rough vegetation for cover, and ideally sunshine for at least the first half of the day.

Constructing the heap is simple. As with a brash pile, start with some woody plant stems or a few branches as a base layer. Next, add leaves, lawn clippings, and wildflower hay in layers. Once you have piled everything up, cover the heap with an offcut of pond liner (or other plastic sheet), and anchor this at the edges with some rocks or logs. Adding this cover makes the heap heat up and "sweat" – accelerating the decomposition process and creating a warm and damp environment – and hides inhabitants away from predators (see also pages 156–59 for a reptile-friendly compost bin). This habitat is perfect for grass snakes to lay their eggs in.

Grass snakes often hunt for amphibians in gardens with wildlife ponds, and the females lay their eggs in June (often in compost heaps). Since the young snakes hatch during August and September, you'll need to leave the heaps undisturbed between late May and September. Any fresh material can be added in October and again in April after any reptiles have emerged from hibernation.

A LOG PILE

Every wildlife garden needs a log pile. They are easy to make and invaluable for wildlife. Site your log pile in a woodland area, at the bottom of a hedge or in a meadow, surrounded by long grass. Choose the wood of native tree species, such as ash, oak, and lime, wherever possible. A log pile needs good contact with the ground, so bury the bottom logs halfway into the soil. This woody habitat attracts specialist beetles, such as the lesser stag beetle, the larvae of which feed on soft, decaying wood.

A Instead of disposing with unwanted garden "waste", use it to create a brash pile. **B** A click beetle spotted roaming a log pile.

Woodlice, centipedes, millipedes, spiders, and worms will all enjoy this cool and damp habitat, too.

There's no need to go for a neat pyramid when stacking logs. You can simply place them randomly but securely on top of one another, ensuring there are gaps for amphibians and small mammals to access the pile. Wood mice and bank voles might soon nest inside the pile. Frogs, toads, and newts also shelter and hibernate there. During the warmer months, you may even find common lizards basking on top of the pile.

A PILE OF STONES

Stone piles (also known as "cairns") are a great way of creating a wildlife habitat from any unwanted stones and pieces of rubble found around the garden. They are particularly good for hibernating reptiles and amphibians. For this reason, site the stone pile near a wildlife pond or in an area of long grass where common lizards, slow worms, and grass snakes naturally dwell.

Start with the largest stones at the bottom and use smaller stones as you build up; for stability, the pile should be narrower at the top. Big or small, in a shady area or in full sunshine, your stone pile will be loved by wildlife all year.

Transform garden and food waste
into a rich compost while offering
up a brilliant and warm habitat for
slow worms and other creatures.

A REPTILE-FRIENDLY
COMPOST BIN

Given how easy it is to turn household and garden waste into compost, it
is baffling why so many people continue to buy plastic bags of the stuff,
especially when much of it contains peat. Peat extraction is responsible for
massive destruction of wild heathland, and results in vast amounts of
carbon being released from these ancient carbon sinks (see page 80).

   Making your own compost couldn't be simpler. All you need is a
ready supply of compostable materials (see page 158) and a bin to put
them in. You can buy your own compost bin, but it isn't too difficult to
make your own. Our rustic-looking design doubles up as a refuge for
heat-seeking reptiles, including slow worms (legless lizards that adore
eating slugs – an efficient form of garden pest control) and grass snakes
(which are non-venomous and are harmless to humans).

Cold-blooded slow worms (above)
and grass snakes (below) will shelter in
the warmth of the compost bin.

BUILDING THE BIN

We made our bin using sheets of corrugated metal. This can be tricky to cut if you've never tried metalwork before (and requires serious eye, ear, and face protection). If you prefer, you can use wooden gravel boards or old pallet wood. Your final bin should be no smaller than 90cm (35in) wide, 60cm (24in) deep, and 100cm (39in) tall; for these dimensions, you'll need to cut two 100 x 60cm (39 x 24in) side panels, and two 90 x 60cm (35 x 24in) panels for the front and back. If you can make it larger, do: bigger compost heaps generate more heat and make for cosier spaces for wildlife to shelter during colder months. The bin shown opposite is around 200 x 100 x 200cm (78 x 39 x 78in) in size, with a half-height front panel to allow for easy access.

Find a scruffy corner of the garden that receives sunshine in the morning. This is crucial for warming the reptiles up before they move around and look for food. Using a post knocker or sledge hammer, knock four stakes into the ground to match the width and depth of your bin, ensuring that they are vertical. Screw the front panel into place (if using metal, you'll want to drill pilot holes first), leaving a gap of at least 7.5cm (3in) at the bottom to give wildlife access to the warm compost. Continue with the remaining panels, placing them flush with the ground and checking regularly with a spirit level to ensure that everything is even. Finally, trim away any excess off the stakes.

MAKING COMPOST

In order for your waste to break down and become compost, you need the right balance of "green" and "brown" waste. A mix of around 25–50 per cent green waste and 50–75 per cent brown waste is ideal. By following the advice shown opposite, it'll take a year or two for your first batch of compost to be ready. Check it each October, when there is little risk of disturbing any young grass snakes (which hatch in August and September) but before other creatures enter hibernation, then turn it over (to mix up the waste) or empty it if it looks ready.

GREEN WASTE YOU CAN ADD:

GRASS CUTTINGS

LEAFY PLANTS

UNCOOKED FOOD WASTE

BROWN WASTE YOU CAN ADD:

HEDGE TRIMMINGS

WOODCHIP

PAPER AND CARDBOARD

1

Fix the corrugated sheets with exterior screws and ensure a 7.5cm (3in) gap between the ground and the bottom of the front panel to allow wildlife access.

2

Start with a good layer of small branches and twigs, letting air into the heap and providing easy gaps for animals to get into the material inside the bin.

3

Add leaves, cut perennial stems, then grass, then more leaves, and so on. As the material decomposes, it shrinks down and begins to generate heat.

4

Use corrugated roofing material or an old piece of roofing felt (black side up) as the "roof" of your heap, ensuring everything is neatly covered.

Nurture a new generation
of birdlife in your garden by
providing them with food, water,
and a place to call home.

BIRD BOXES
AND FEEDERS

One of the most wonderful moments from our childhood was when our dad made a wooden nest box and nailed it to the old apple tree in the garden. The very same afternoon, we were overjoyed to see a pair of blue tits investigating the new box. In and out they went, a little face occasionally peeping out of the hole. One bird spent ages pecking at the entrance hole and, when the pair eventually flew off together, we knew that we had to put up more nesting boxes for other birds.

Older buildings tend to offer generous nesting opportunities for birds – starlings behind old fascia boards, great tits in stone walls, or housemartins in eaves, for instance. But take a walk around an average town or housing estate, and it doesn't take long to realize just how hard our hole-nesting bird species have it these days. It's simple – we need more bird-nesting sites.

Surrounded by hawthorn, this nest box
is perfectly positioned for its blue tit
inhabitants, with plenty of cover nearby.

A range of different types of bird boxes are available online, including specialist ones for species such as treecreepers and owls. Alternatively, you could make your own; we've provided instructions for a simple box below. Whatever you choose, simply secure them to a wall or tree around January (before nesting begins in earnest).

BUILDING A BIRD BOX

First, decide which bird species you can potentially attract. It is perhaps a bit ambitious to erect an osprey platform beside your small wildlife pond in the centre of a city, but you could definitely consider boxes for blue and great tits, starlings, robins, and wrens. Use the table on page 186 to determine what box to use and where to position it; check the RSPB's website for bird box dimensions. Construct boxes from sustainably sourced timber – we've found pressure-treated gravel board is perfect. For standard small-hole nest boxes, we use boards 15cm wide and 2.5cm deep (6 x 1in); for larger boxes, use 20 x 2.5cm (8 x 1in) boards. Untreated softwood also works well, but will deteriorate faster with the weather, so would need to be treated.

We tend to use 50mm x 4mm exterior wood screws for construction as these last for years and make it easy to take the box apart in the future. Use a good-quality, outdoor black T-hinge for the roof or simply screw it down. As long as the nest box is draught free and fairly weatherproof, the birds will be absolutely fine. Finally, drill a few 5mm (³⁄₁₆in) drainage holes in the base of the box.

> To see a blue tit foraging for caterpillars in trees you have planted, and raise young from a nest box is wonderful.

A We sited this box on a north-facing tree. **B** House sparrows are communal birds and nest close to each other so we put up colony boxes. **C** These cup nests in the eaves are used by house martins – this colony is now home to 14 pairs. **D** This natural box is made from a coppiced hazel and attracts blue, great, and coal tits.

LOCATING A BIRD BOX

Always site your boxes facing somewhere between north and east, ensuring any nestlings will not overheat in the hottest part of the day, and keep well out of reach of cats. When it comes to fixing your boxes in their final position, use screws and wall plugs on brick and stone buildings, and either screws or soft nails when fixing to trees. We use a large nail hammered in with about 2.5cm (1in) protruding, allowing for the tree to grow and push the box outwards along the nail.

Cats are the biggest threat of all to garden birds. Make sure all bird boxes and feeding stations are safely out of paw's reach.

If positioned well, it shouldn't be too long before your new box has some occupants. Don't disturb the birds during the breeding season, particularly once nest building stops, as the females will probably be incubating eggs. Once food is regularly being taken into the box, you know the young are feeding well. After the young have fledged, leave the box until the autumn, to make sure any roosting birds have left for good. Then, remove the old nesting material as it will probably be housing some parasites, such as fleas.

POSITIONING AND FILLING FEEDERS

When it comes to feeding birds, location is everything. No bird will come to a feeder placed in the middle of an open and featureless plot. To encourage birds to visit, you'll need to site a feeder where a bird can hop safely from a nearby shrub or tree and then fly off without the risk of attack from a predator, including cats. Species such as hawthorn, dog rose, and holly are all excellent for providing safe refuge (see pages 52–57).

Place feeders within 2m (6½ft) of planting cover, and it is even better if there are a few taller shrubs and trees nearby. The ideal set up is to have a mature tree, such as a silver birch or alder, with maybe a smaller apple tree

A By putting out niger seed, you may attract bramblings.
B House sparrows love to feast on fat balls.

or rowan adjacent, to bring the birds down through the canopy layers, towards the dense cover and feeding station.

With the exact location decided, you need to think about what to put in the feeder. The best general advice is to buy a good-quality seed feeder and fill it with a mixture with a high content of sunflower hearts as well as other seeds, such as red and white millet, canary seed, kibbled maize, pinhead oats, and oil seed rape. Such a mix will offer a varied diet to the many potential bird species that might visit. Good-quality peanuts are excellent for many birds, and a real favourite of great spotted woodpeckers, nuthatches, and tits. These nuts give the birds a boost when they need the energy in the autumn and winter months. When it comest to fat balls, we opt for vegan versions as we feel that it's not ethical to feed birds animal-based products. Another important winter food is fallen apples, as thrushes, such as fieldfare, redwing, and blackbirds, really enjoy these in the harsh winter weather. All feeders need cleaning every three months or so.

Finally, offer a regular clean supply of water for birds to drink and bathe in; if you don't have a pond, simply fill a shallow dish or birdbath.

Insects do such valuable work, pollinating flowers and providing food. No wildlife garden is complete without an insect hotel.

INSECT HOTELS

Rarely a week goes by without more news of the large-scale decline of insects, especially pollinators like bees. The threats of habitat loss, climate change, and intensive agriculture have led to nearly 10 per cent of wild bee species in Europe facing extinction. Naturally, we feel we must do something to help reverse this potentially devastating situation, and one of the simplest and fastest ways you can help is by providing insects with a safe, purpose-built home – otherwise known as an "insect hotel".

The basic principle behind an insect hotel is to use different materials to create a variety of habitats for a wide range of insect species. Most hotels feature an assortment of holes that vary in diameter from 2 to 10mm (1/16–3/8in), depending on the species the hotel is intended to attract. Our hotels appeal to solitary bees, such as red mason bees and leaf-cutter bees, along with other insects (see page 169).

This compact, multi-purpose insect hotel features a variety of habitats designed to appeal to a range of invertebrates.

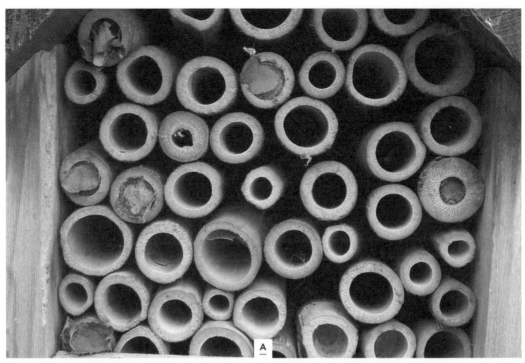

CLASSIC CANE BOX

The simplest method is to build a basic bird box (see pages 160–165), but leave the front off. Stack the box with cut bamboo canes or hollow plant stems from species such as hogweed and teasel. Position the box on a south-facing wall at least 1m (3ft) off the ground so that it gets the sun.

COB BLOCK

Cob, an ancient building material (a mix of clay, sharp sand, straw, and water) is an ideal material for making bee hotels. Experiment with the ratio of materials until you get the right mixture. Push the thick, sticky mixture into an open-fronted bird box or similar container. Insert variously sized canes, sticks, or anything 2–10mm (1/16–3/8in) in diameter into the cob, and leave to dry. Once the cob mixture hardens, remove the objects to reveal the nesting chambers. Fix the cob block at least 1m (3ft) off the ground in a sunny position.

CUSTOMIZED HABITATS...

HOLE-NESTING BEES – canes, plant stems, and holes made in wood and cob

LADYBIRDS – sticks, straw, and dry leaves

LACEWINGS – corrugated cardboard

EARWIGS – fir cones (keep in place with some wire netting)

SMALL SPIDERS – slates and tiles

STANDING LOGS

Gather together some large logs or sections of tree trunk in a sunny and sheltered spot. The logs should vary in length from 1.2 to 2.4m (4–8ft) and be 10–30cm (4–12in) in diameter. Bury the bottom third of each log in the ground, back fill with soil, and compact it so it is stable. Then drill lots of 2–10mm (1/16–3/8in) holes, angled slightly downwards so rain can't fill the nesting chambers. Standing logs will attract solitary wasps and bees.

LOOKING AFTER INSECT HOTELS

Clean and maintain these insect habitats to keep them parasite-free. Replace bamboo sticks, plant stems, and cob blocks every couple of years. Drill extra holes every year in standing logs and replace the logs after a few years.

A Leaf-cutter bees have filled the ends of several canes. **B** This hotel features a mixture of drilled logs, fir cones, and canes.

A garden is a busy place during the hours of darkness. Don't forget to provide bats with a place to rest and food to eat.

BAT BOXES

Lovers of wildlife ponds, coppice belts, and woodlands, bats are otherworldly and incredible. Over the years that we have been creating ponds for wildlife, the very same day we fill up the pond (or the same night rather), as if by magic bats appear.

The species seen most often over wildlife ponds is the common pipistrelle. This tiny, furry mammal, weighing around 3–8g (1/10–1/4oz), is capable of consuming 3,000 insects in a single night. These amazing nocturnal "hoovers" will make short work of any insect brave enough to enter the airspace above your pond, mosquitoes included.

Bats are highly adaptable; they can be found in urban gardens as frequently as in the countryside, using linear features such as avenues of trees, hedgerows along housing estates, and sections of canal to navigate around town. But one of the biggest problems facing bats, particularly in urban areas, is a lack of suitable roosting sites. That's where we can help.

These Kent-style bat boxes, secured beneath the roof of an urban home, can each provide a refuge for up to six bats.

A BAT-FRIENDLY GARDEN

It's easy to forget about bats when planning a wildlife garden since they don't get as much press as hedgehogs and bumblebees. But creating roosting sites for bats is simple and highly effective. Our most successful bat roost is in urban Hertfordshire, UK, where bats hadn't been seen for 20 years. We added a couple of wildlife ponds, meadows, native planting, and, of course, clusters of bat boxes to the garden – and common pipistrelles returned within six months. Their numbers have since increased year on year, despite being in the centre of a busy town, close to a main road. It really can be a case of "if you build it, they will come…"

If you could put up a bat box or plant flowers, such as night-scented stock and honeysuckle, that attract moths for the bats to feed on (see pages 182–86), bats would be much more widespread. And bats offer an excuse for you to spend the night out in your wildlife garden, too.

BUILDING A BAT BOX

If you have the space and ability to do so, installing a bat box or two on your property would give your local bat population a welcome boost. Bats love to squeeze into tight, thin cavities, where there is no draught and they can remain warm with minimal effort. We recommend a "Kent-style" bat box, which can be ordered online, but is also easy to make.

To build your own bat box, you'll need to use planks of rough-sawn, untreated wood. It is vital to use wood that hasn't been treated because some preservatives can be harmful, or even fatal, to bat species. By using wood with a rough surface, you're providing the bats with something to grip onto. Larch is good, and can usually be sourced direct from timber mills. Failing this, untreated pine will be fine, but will need roughing up on the surfaces the bats will be crawling up.

While dimensions for your bat box can vary, see the Bat Conservation Trust website for some examples, it is important to get the size of the opening right. The cavity should be between 15 and 20mm (½–¾in) wide. Any smaller and they probably won't fit; any wider and they won't be happy, because bats hate draughts.

Bats like to roost together, so it's good practice to put up a cluster of bat boxes with differing cavity sizes. The Kent-style design also allows two or

A Each slim gap in the Kent-style box will become home to several tiny bats. **B** If you have mature trees in your garden, brown long-eared bats may make it their home.

even three cavities within one bat box, allowing the bats to move around to get comfy. Should you wish to go one step further, you can purchase ready-made boxes designed to be built into the house itself, embedded in the brickwork. This is a great way of offering a permanent home for the bats where they have greater shelter through the colder months and more extreme weather.

LOCATING BAT BOXES

Position your bat boxes on an outer wall of your house. Choose a wall that gets the most sun, facing south or west. Boxes should be located as high as possible (above 4m/13ft), just below the eaves or overhang of the roof, for best results. Group as many boxes together as you wish to give the bats more options and more room as their numbers build over time.

Follow nature's lead and provide a stony habitat to offer a superb and safe home for birds, frogs, lizards, and bank voles.

A DRY STONE WALL

All over the world, "dry stone walls" – built only from stone, with no mortar – often mark field boundaries, churchyards, and retaining walls on slopes. These stone walls come in a wonderful array of shapes, sizes, and colours, many of which are peculiar to an area, using locally quarried stone.

Good walls become better with age; the more that vegetation is able to colonize them, the more animals can use them as a refuge. One of the best features of dry stone walls is the fact that they are linear, allowing wildlife the chance to move safely along these corridors.

In a garden, you can plan and build a small section of wall – a couple of courses (rows) of stones will work; even a simple pile of stones will do (see page 155). What is important is the many small gaps between the stones, which are perfect for providing a home for a broad range of animals and plants. Site these mini-walls beside nectar borders, behind a pond, or as a "step up" between two areas of meadow in a sloped garden.

Plants such as white stonecrop love nooks and crannies just as much as spiders and insects do.

BUILDING THE WALL

Once you've chosen the location for the dry stone wall, you'll need to source the stone. If you're lucky, you may have plenty lying around your plot; if not, you will have to buy some from a reclamation yard or quarry.

To build a section of wall, build two parallel rows of large stones on the ground, dug slightly into the soil. Place the stones so that they are level and all at the same height. Ideally, use larger stones at the base and slowly work up, placing ever-smaller stones as you build the stack.

As your mini-wall takes shape, infill the central cavity with the smallest stones; this allows access for animals. Then, as you build up, switch to a mix of stony soil and sand for the infill; it is soft enough for amphibians and reptiles to squeeze into and hibernate. The interior of these stony places remains at a constant coolness and humidity, ideal for common lizards and toads.

Once you have finished, fill the larger joints, ideally with some subsoil (topsoil in small amounts is fine). Then, choose species from the plant list on pages 182–86 to colonize your wall and buy them as large plug plants, as smaller plugs can quickly die off if they're not watered regularly.

WHO LIVES THERE

It is remarkable how many species use these walls in gardens. Great tits and blue tits regularly nest in them, and wrens love to hunt through them looking for spiders. Wood mice and bank voles adore the nooks and crannies. Frogs and toads will rest at the base of these stones, and various newts hibernate in such places. Grass snakes, adders, slow worms, and common lizards enjoy basking and using these places; often the highest concentrations of lizards in a garden will be found on and close to dry stone walls.

YOU COULD HELP...

BANK VOLE

BLUE TIT

COMMON FROG

COMMON LIZARD

COMMON TOAD

GRASS SNAKE

GREAT TIT

SLOW WORM

SMOOTH NEWT

WREN

A White stonecrop B Herb Robert
C Maidenhair spleenwort

A striking display of logs can also benefit your garden's web of life, starting with the creepy crawlies who love the dead wood.

A LOG WALL

If you are looking to screen an unsightly shed or garage, or perhaps create a secluded "room" for relaxation within your plot, you can do it in a slightly more formal way, while still providing a much-needed home for wildlife, by creating a log wall. As its name suggests, this project involves cutting sections of logs to size and stacking them into a bookcase-type frame, to create a deadwood habitat able to host a myriad of invertebrates. While it is more ambitious than a simple log pile (see pages 154–55) or even a standing-log insect hotel (see page 169), the design shows off the beauty of the logs and proves that a wild garden can still look aesthetically pleasing.

BUILDING THE LOG WALL

You can make this log wall any size you like and in any location. Since the design is encased within a wooden frame, you can choose to site it within

We incorporated a hollow frame in this living trellis screen to hold a large stack of logs, as a formal alternative to a log pile.

an existing fence (see pages 46–51), against a garage wall, or even as a feature near a seating area, as shown in the picture on page 179. This is a heavy-duty project so if you are feeling daunted, you may prefer to call in the professionals, see page 192.

First, you will need to dig holes for two fence posts. These holes should be suffciently deep so that the posts are secure. Insert the posts and, ensuring that they are held firmly upright, concrete them in up to ground level. This stage is essential in order to make a free-standing wall: the posts will effectively act as retaining walls, as they will hold the heavy stack of logs in place. If you site your wall against an existing wall, such as the side of a garage, you may not need to concrete in the posts as you could fix them to the existing structure instead. Check that you own any structure you are attaching your log wall to, or that you have permission.

> A well-made log wall can last for a decade or more.

Once the posts are firmly in place, it's time to create the frame. Measure the distance between the two posts, and cut two wooden planks – for the top and bottom – to fit this space. Then, you'll need more planks for the sides of the frame. Old scaffolding timbers, around 20 x 5cm (8 x 2in) are ideal for these frame pieces. Lastly, you'll need two 20cm- (8in-) long logs.

Set the logs upright beneath where the frame will sit. These "legs" will stop the frame bowing under the weight of the stacked logs later on. Place the bottom shelf on top of the upright logs, and secure in place with two right-angled brackets on the underside of each side to offer extra support.

Next, set the side pieces against the posts and secure them in place with heavy-duty exterior screws. (At this stage, if you want to create a back to the log wall for privacy – or to help contain the logs more securely – screw a sheet of exterior-grade plywood, cut to size, to the frame.)

Now, you're ready to add the logs. Unless you have a ready supply of logs to cut up, ask a local tree surgeon for any spare logs or wood that you can cut up. You could also get in touch with your local wildlife trust; if they undertake coppicing, they may well have some logs going spare. You'll need a random selection of logs, up to about 25cm (10in) in diameter. Enjoy the jigsaw puzzle-like activity of completing the empty space and work all the way up to the top; fill the gaps with smaller logs.

Before long, invertebrates will begin to explore the deadwood habitat of the log wall, including centipedes, millipedes, woodlouse spiders, and even stag beetles. This resident population will, in turn, attract birds looking to feed on them.

LOOKING AFTER A LOG WALL

Because the log wall is sat off the ground, it will last over a decade, although the duration does depend a bit on what species of log you use; softwoods, such as pine, won't last as long as hardwoods, such as oak and ash, which could last up to 20 years.

As the logs in your wall age, they become home to all sorts of invertebrates, including woodlice, many species of beetle, and spiders. Once the older logs have deteriorated, simply replace them with new ones to maintain your log wall over the years.

PLANT LISTS

This appendix lists a core selection of wildlife-friendly plants by chapter and project, so you can see which species would work well in different situations. Each plant is listed by its common name and its scientific name.

TREES AND SHRUBS (SEE PAGES 28–57)

These trees and shrubs are all suitable for supporting wildlife. Work out which species will work best in your garden based on their eventual size. All species, with the exception of Scots pine, can be coppiced.

SMALL TREES AND SHRUBS

Small trees reach 2–5m (6½–16½ft) in height. Most shrubs will grow to around 2m (6½ft) in height; a small shrub would be 1.2–1.8m (4–6ft), a medium shrub 1.8–2.4m (6–8ft), and a large shrub would be 2.4–3m (8–10ft).

Alder buckthorn (*Frangula alnus*)
Barberry (*Berberis vulgaris*)
Blackthorn (*Prunus spinosa*)
Box (*Buxus sempervirens*)
Bramble (*Rubus fruticosus*)
Bullace (wild plum) (*Prunus domestica*)
Butterfly bush (buddleja) (*Buddleja davidii*)
Common gorse (*Ulex europaea*)
Crab apple (*Malus sylvestris*)
Dog rose (*Rosa canina*)
Dogwood (*Cornus sanguinea*)
Elder (*Sambucus nigra*)
Field rose (*Rosa arvensis*)
Guelder rose (*Viburnum opulus*)
Hawthorn (*Crataegus monogyna*)
Hazel (*Corylus avellana*)
Holly (*Ilex aquifolium*)
Purging buckthorn (*Rhamnus cathartica*)
Spindle (*Euonymus europaea*)
Wayfaring tree (*Viburnum lantana*)
Whitebeam (*Sorbus aria*)
Wild privet (*Ligustrum vulgare*)
Yew (*Taxus baccata*)

MEDIUM-SIZED TREES AND SHRUBS

Such sized trees would measure 5–15m (16½–50ft).

Bird cherry (*Prunus padus*)
Bullace (wild plum) (*Prunus domestica*)
Crab apple (*Malus sylvestris*)
Field maple (*Acer campestre*)
Goat willow (*Salix caprea*)
Hawthorn (*Crataegus monogyna*)
Hazel (*Corylus avellane*)
Holly (*Ilex aquifolium*)
Rowan (*Sorbus aucuparia*)
Wild cherry (*Prunus avium*)
Wild pear (*Pyrus pyraster*)
Wild service (*Sorbus torminalis*)
Wych elm (*Ulmus glabra*)
Yew (*Taxus baccata*)

LARGE TREES

For guidance, large trees measure roughly 15–35m (50–115ft) in height.

Alder (*Alnus glutinosa*)
Ash (*Fraxinus excelsior*)
Aspen (*Populus tremula*)
Beech (*Fagus sylvatica*)
Black poplar (*Populus nigra*)
Crack willow (*Salix fragilis*)
Downy birch (*Betula pubescens*)
English elm (*Ulmus procera*)
European larch (*Larix decidua*)
Hornbeam (*Carpinus betulus*)
Horse chestnut (*Aesculus hippocastanum*)
Large-leaved lime (*Tilia platyphyllos*)
Pedunculate oak (*Quercus robur*)
Scots pine (*Pinus sylvestris*)
Silver birch (*Betula pendula*)
Small-leaved lime (*Tilia cordata*)
Sweet chestnut (*Castanea sativa*)
White willow (*Salix alba*)
Wild service (*Sorbus torminalis*)
Wych elm (*Ulmus glabra*)

CLIMBERS

Dog rose (*Rosa canina*)
Field rose (*Rosa arvensis*)
Firethorn (*Pyracantha coccinea*)
Hops (*Humulus lupulus*)
Ivy (*Hedera helix*)
Jasmine (*Jasminum officinale*)
Thornless bramble (*Rubus fructicosus* 'Merton thornless')
Wild clematis (*Clematis vitalba*)
Wild honeysuckle (*Lonicera periclymenum*)

WILDLIFE PONDS (SEE PAGES 58–91)

All plants are suitable in moderation for small ponds except those with *, which are only suitable for large ponds. For a successful pond, whatever the size, choose at least three different types of pond plants from each category below.

FLOATING AQUATIC PLANTS

Broad-leaved pondweed (Potamogeton natans)
Fringed water lily (Nymphoides peltatum)
Frogbit (Limnobium laevigatum)
Water soldier (Stratiotes aloides)
White water lily* (Nymphaea alba)
Yellow water lily* (Nuphar lutea)

GRASSES, REEDS, RUSHES, AND SEDGES

Branched bur-reed* (Sparganium erectum)
Common clubrush* (Schoenoplectus lacustris)
Common reed* (Phragmites australis)
Cotton-grass (Eriophorum angustifolium)
False fox sedge (Carex otrubae)
Glaucous sedge (Carex flacca)
Hard rush (Juncus inflexus)
Hop sedge (Carex lupuliformis)
Jointed rush (Juncus articulates)
Lesser pond sedge (Carex acutiformis)
Pendulous sedge* (Carex pendula)
Saw sedge* (Gahnia aspera)
Soft rush (Juncus effuses)
Sweet galingale* (Cyperus longus)
Tufted hairgrass (Deschampsia cespitosa)

MARGINAL AQUATIC PLANTS

Amphibious bistort (Persicaria amphibia)
Arrowhead (Sagittaria sagittifolia)
Bogbean (Menyanthes trifoliata)
Brooklime (Veronica beccabunga)
Flowering rush (Butomus umbellatus)
Marsh marigold (Caltha palustris)
Water mint (Mentha aquatica)
Water plantain (Alisma plantago-aquatica)
Yellow flag iris* (Iris pseudacorus)

OXYGENATING PLANTS

Curled pondweed (Potamogeton crispus)
Hornwort (Ceratophyllum demersum)
Spiked water milfoil (Myriophyllum spicatum)
Water crowfoot (Ranunculus aquatilis)
Water starwort (Callitriche stagnalis)
Water violet (Hottonia palustris)

DAMP-LOVING PLANTS

All the plants in this list are suited to damp conditions and are ideal for the planted margins around a pond and for a bog garden. Plants with ** are suited to the specialized conditions of a peat bog (see p.80).

Bilberry** (Vaccinium myrtillus)
Bugle (Ajuga reptans)
Common fleabane (Pulicaria dysenterica)
Common valerian (Valeriana officinalis)
Cotton-grass** (Eriophorum angustifolium)
Creeping Jenny (Lysimachia nummularia)
Cross-leaved heath** (Erica tetralix)
Cuckooflower (Cardamine pratensis)
Devil's-bit scabious (Succisa pratensis)
Great burnet (Sanguisorba officinalis)
Greater bird's-foot trefoil (Lotus pedunculatus)
Gypsywort (Lycopus europaeus)
Hemp agrimony (Eupatorium cannabinum)
Lesser spearwort (Ranunculus flammula)
Marsh mallow (Althaea officinalis)
Marsh woundwort (Stachys palustris)
Meadowsweet (Filipendula ulmaria)
Purple loosestrife (Lythrum salicaria)
Purple moor-grass** (Molinia caerulea)
Ragged robin (Lychnis flos-cuculi)
Skullcap (Scutellaria galericulata)
Sneezewort (Achillea ptarmica)
Square-stemmed St John's wort (Hypericum tetrapterum)
Water avens (Geum rivale)
Water figwort (Scrophularia umbrosa)
Water forget-me-not (Myosotis scorpioides)
Yellow loosestrife (Lysimachia vulgaris)

NECTAR BORDERS (SEE PAGES 92–111)

Maximize the nectar available to a wide variety of insects and pollinators by planting a great selection of the following plants.

A NECTAR BORDER

Anise hyssop (Agastache foeniculum)
Aster (Aster x frikartii 'Mönch')
Aubretia (Aubrieta 'Axcent deep purple')
Bird's-foot trefoil (Lotus corniculatus)
Bluebell (Hyacinthoides non-scripta)
Borage (Borago officinalis)
Butterfly bush (buddleja) (Buddleja davidii)
Bugle (Ajuga reptans)
Catmint (Nepeta gigantea 'Six Hills Giant')
Common comfrey (Symphytum officinale)
Common fleabane (Pulicaria dysenterica)
Common knapweed (Centaurea nigra)
Cowslip (Primula veris)
Cuckooflower (Cardamine pratensis)
Dame's violet (Hesperis matronalis)
Devil's-bit scabious (Succisa pratensis)

Field forget-me-not (*Myosotis arvensis*)
Field scabious (*Knautia arvensis*)
Foxglove (*Digitalis purpurea*)
Garlic mustard (*Alliaria petiolate*)
Globe thistle (*Echinops bannaticus*)
Greater knapweed (*Centaurea scabiosa*)
Hebe (*Hebe* 'Midsummer Beauty')
Hedge bedstraw (*Galium mollugo*)
Hellebore (stinking) (*Helleborus foetidus*)
Hemp agrimony (*Eupatorium cannabinum*)
Hollyhock (*Alcea rosea*)
Honesty (*Lunaria annua*)
Hyssop (*Hyssopus officinalis*)
Jacob's ladder (*Polemonium caeruleum*)
Lady's bedstraw (*Galium verum*)
Lavender (*Lavandula angustifolia* 'Hidcote')
Lesser calamint (*Calamintha nepeta*)
Lungwort (*Pulmonaria officinalis*)
Marjoram (*Origanum majorana*)
Meadow cranesbill (*Geranium pratense*)
Nettle leaved bellflower (*Campanula trachelium*)
Ox-eye daisy (*Leucanthemum vulgare*)
Pennyroyal (mint) (*Mentha pulegium*)
Perennial sweetpea (*Lathyrus latifolius*)
Phlox (*Phlox paniculata*)
Primrose (*Primula vulgaris*)
Purple coneflower (*Echinacea purpurea*)
Purple loosestrife (*Lythrum salicaria*)
Ragged robin (*Lychnis flos-cuculi*)
Red campion (*Silene dioica*)
Red clover (*Trifolium pratense*)
Red valerian (*Centranthus ruber*)
Salvia (*Salvia nemerosa* 'Caradonna')
Sedum (*Hylotelephium* 'Autumn Joy')
Self-heal (*Prunella vulgaris*)
Snowdrop (*Galanthus nivalis*)
Tansy (*Tanacetum vulgare*)
Teasel (*Dipsacus fullonum*)
Thyme (*Thymus vulgaris*)
Valerian (*Valeriana officinalis*)
Verbena (*Verbena bonariensis*)
Viper's bugloss (*Echium vulgare*)
Wallflower (*Erysimum* 'Bowles Mauve')
Wild garlic (*Allium ursinum*)
Winter-flowering heather (*Erica carnea*)
Yarrow (*Achillea millefolium*)

A LIMESTONE AND CHALK BANK

Bird's-foot trefoil (*Lotus corniculatus*)
Clustered bellflower (*Campanula glomerate*)
Common rock-rose (*Helianthemum nummalarium*)
Common spotted-orchid (*Dactylorhiza fuchsia*)
Common toadflax (*Linaria vulgaris*)
Dark mullein (*Verbascum nigrum*)
Dropwort (*Filipendula vulgaris*)
Field scabious (*Knautia arvensis*)
Great mullein (*Verbascum thapsus*)
Greater knapweed (*Centaurea scabiosa*)
Harebell (*Campanula rotundifolia*)

Hedge bedstraw (*Galium mollugo*)
Hoary plantain (*Plantago media*)
Horseshoe vetch (*Hippocrepis comosa*)
Kidney vetch (*Anthyllis vulneraria*)
Knapweed (*Centaurea nigra*)
Lady's bedstraw (*Galium verum*)
Meadow cranesbill (*Geranium pratense*)
Nettle-leaved bellflower (*Campanula trachelium*)
Perforate St John's wort (*Hypericum perforatum*)
Quaking grass (*Briza media*)
Rough hawkbit (*Leontodon hispidus*)
Sainfoin (*Onobrychis viciifolia*)
Sheep's fescue (*Festuca ovina*)
Slender-creeping red-fescue (*Festuca rubra*)
Small scabious (*Scabiosa columbaria*)
Smaller cat's-tail (*Phleum bertolonii*)
Spiny restharrow (*Ononis spinosa*)
Vervain (*Verbena officinalis*)
Viper's bugloss (*Echium vulgare*)
Wild basil (*Clinopodium vulgare*)
Wild marjoram (*Origanum vulgare*)
Yellow oat-grass (*Trisetum flavescens*)

WILDFLOWER MEADOWS

(SEE PAGES 112–147)

Different plant species thrive in different types of soil and meadow location, so sow or plant the following species based on your situation.

A PERENNIAL WILDFLOWER MEADOW

Agrimony (*Agrimonia eupatoria*)
Autumn hawkbit (*Scorzoneroides autumnalis*)
Betony (*Stachys officinalis*)
Bird's-foot trefoil (*Lotus corniculatus*)
Bladder campion (*Silene vulgaris*)
Common knapweed (*Centaurea nigra*)
Common sorrel (*Rumex acetosa*)
Common toadflax (*Linaria vulgaris*)
Cowslip (*Primula veris*)
Dark mullein (*Verbascum nigrum*)
Devil's-bit scabious (*Succisa pratensis*)
Field scabious (*Knautia arvensis*)
Great mullein (*Verbascum thapsus*)
Greater knapweed (*Centaurea scabiosa*)
Hedge bedstraw (*Galium mollugo*)
Hoary plantain (*Plantago media*)
Kidney vetch (*Anthyllis vulneraria*)
Lady's bedstraw (*Galium verum*)
Meadow buttercup (*Ranunculus acris*)
Meadow clary (*Salvia pratensis*)
Meadow vetchling (*Lathyrus pratensis*)
Musk mallow (*Malva moschata*)
Ox-eye daisy (*Leucanthemum vulgare*)
Ragged robin (*Silene flos-cuculi*)
Red campion (*Silene dioica*)
Red clover (*Trifolium pratense*)

Rough hawkbit (*Leontodon hispidus*)
Sainfoin (*Onobrychis viciifolia*)
Salad burnet (*Poterium sanguisorba*)
Self-heal (*Prunella vulgaris*)
Small scabious (*Scabiosa columbaria*)
Sneezewort (*Achillea ptarmica*)
Spiny restharrow (*Ononis spinosa*)
Teasel (*Dipsacus fullonum*)
Tufted vetch (*Vicia cracca*)
Viper's bugloss (*Echium vulgare*)
White campion (*Silene latifolia*)
Wild basil (*Clinopodium vulgare*)
Wild carrot (*Daucus carota*)
Wild clary (*Salvia verbenaca*)
Wild marjoram (*Origanum vulgare*)
Wild mignonette (*Reseda lutea*)
Wild parsnip (*Pastinaca sativa*)
Yarrow (*Achillea millefolium*)
Yellow rattle (*Rhinanthus minor*)

A CORNFIELD ANNUAL MEADOW

Black-eyed Susan (*Rudbeckia hirta*)
Common poppy (*Papaver rhoeas*)
Corn chamomile (*Anthemis austriaca*)
Corn marigold (*Glebionis segetum*)
Corncockle (*Agrostemma githago*)
Cornflower (*Centaurea cyanus*)
Night-scented stock (*Matthiola longipetala*)
Poached egg plant (*Limnanthes douglasii*)

A FLOWERING LAWN

Bird's-foot trefoil (*Lotus corniculatus*)
Black medick (*Medicago lupulina*)
Cat's ears (*Hypochaeris radicata*)
Cowslip (*Primula veris*)
Daisy (*Bellis perennis*)
Dandelion (*Taraxacum officinale*)
Lady's bedstraw (*Galium verum*)
Meadow buttercup (*Ranunculus acris*)
Ox-eye daisy (*Leucanthemum vulgare*)
Primrose (*Primula vulgaris*)
Red clover (*Trifolium pratense*)
Rough hawkbit (*Leontodon hispidus*)
Sainfoin (*Onobrychis viciifolia*)
Self-heal (*Prunella vulgaris*)
Sorrel (*Rumex acetosa*)
Yarrow (*Achillea millefolium*)

SHADE-LOVING PLANTS

These plant species are ideal for a woodland glade, but can also be a good option for any shady areas of the garden. Bulbs are indicated with *.

Betony (*Stachys officinalis*)
Bluebell* (*Hyacinthoides non-scripta*)
Cowslip (*Primula veris*)
Dog-violet (*Viola riviniana*)

Foxglove (*Digitalis purpurea*)
Garlic mustard (*Alliaria petiolate*)
Greater stitchwort (*Stellaria holostea*)
Lesser celandine* (*Ficaria verna*)
Nettle-leaved bellflower (*Campanula trachelium*)
Primrose (*Primula vulgaris*)
Red campion (*Silene dioica*)
Self-heal (*Prunella vulgaris*)
Snowdrop (*Galanthus nivalis*)
Stinking hellebore (*Helleborus foetidus*)
Stinking iris (*Iris foetidissima*)
Sweet violet (*Viola odorata*)
Sweet woodruff* (*Galium odoratum*)
Wild daffodil* (*Narcissus pseudonarcissus*)
Wild garlic* (*Allium ursinum*)
Wood anemone* (*Anemone nemorosa*)
Wood cranesbill (*Geranium sylvaticum*)
Wood sage (*Teucrium scorodonia*)
Wood sorrel* (*Oxalis acetosella*)

WELCOME MORE WILDLIFE

(SEE PAGES 148–181)

Encourage bats to visit with planting, as well as bat boxes. Choose plants from the list overleaf to colonize a dry stone wall and use large plug plants.

PLANTING FOR BATS

Spring flowers:
Bluebell (*Hyacinthoides non-scripta*)
Cuckooflower (*Cardamine pratensis*)
Dandelion (*Taraxacum officinale*)
False rock cress (*Aubreita deltoidea*)
Field forget-me-not (*Myosotis arvensis*)
Goat willow (*Salix caprea*)
Honesty (*Lunaria annua*)
Ox-eye daisy (*Leucanthemum vulgare*)
Pansy (*Viola tricolor* var. *hortensis*)
Primrose (*Primula vulgaris*)
Red campion (*Silene dioica*)
Red clover (*Trifolium pratense*)
Sweet rocket (Dame's violet) (*Hesperis matronalis*)
Wallflower (*Erysimum* 'Bowles Mauve')
White campion (*Silene latifolia*)

Summer flowers:
Bladder campion (*Silene vulgaris*)
Buddleja (*Buddleja davidii*)
Common valerian (*Valeriana officinalis*)
Evening primrose (*Oenothera biennis*)
Field scabious (*Knautia arvensis*)
French marigold (*Tagetes erecta*)
Hebe (*Hebe* 'Midsummer Beauty')
Hemp agrimony (*Eupatorium cannabinum*)
Jasmine (*Jasminum officinale*)
Knapweed (*Centaurea nigra*)
Lavender (*Lavandula angustifolia* 'Hidcote')
Marjoram (*Origanum majorana*)

Night-scented stock (*Matthiola longipetala*)
Red valerian (*Centranthus ruber*)
Salvia (*Salvia nemerosa 'Caradonna'*)
Sweet rocket (Dame's violet) (*Hesperis matronalis*)
Thyme (*Thymus vulgaris*)
Tobacco plants (*Nicotiana alata* and *Nicotiana sylvestris*)
Verbena (*Verbena bonariensis*)
Wild honeysuckle (*Lonicera periclymenum*)
Wild mint (*Mentha arvensis*)
Wild privet (*Ligustrum vulgare*)

Autumn flowers:
Ivy (*Hedera helix*)
Michaelmas daisy (*Aster amellus*)
Sedum (*Hylotelephium 'Autumn Joy'*)

A DRY STONE WALL

Biting stonecrop (*Sedum acre*)
Common rock-rose (*Helianthemum nummularium*)
Dark mullein (*Verbascum nigrum*)
False rock cress (*Aubrieta deltoidea*)
Foxglove (*Digitalis purpurea*)
Greater celandine (*Chelidonium majus*)
Harebell (*Campanula rotundifolia*)
Herb robert (*Geranium robertianum*)
Ivy-leaved toadflax (*Cymbalaria muralis*)
Kidney vetch (*Anthyllis vulneraria*)
Orpine (*Sedum telephium*)
Red valerian (*Centranthus ruber*)
Reflexed stonecrop (*Sedum reflexum*)
Sheep's-bit (*Jasione montana*)
Thrift (*Armeria maritima*)
Toadflax (*Linaria vulgaris*)
Welsh poppy (*Meconopsis cambrica*)
Wild thyme (*Thymus polytrichus*)

BIRD BOXES

Use the following table to determine which bird box to use and where to position it.

THE RIGHT BIRD BOX FOR THE RIGHT BIRD

SPECIES	BOX TYPE	HOLE SIZE	BOX LOCATION	BOX POSITION ABOVE GROUND
Blue tit	Small-hole	2.5cm (1in)	Trees and buildings	2.4m (7¾ft) and above
Coal tit	Small-hole	2.5cm (1in)	Trees (coniferous)	Ground level and above
Great tit	Small-hole	2.5cm (1in)	Trees, buildings	2.4m (7¾ft) and above
House martin	Cup-shape	Approx. 6cm (2⅓in)	Buildings	Directly under eaves/roof
House sparrow	Small-hole	3.2cm (1¼in)	Buildings	Gutter height, adjacent to roof overhang
Pied wagtail	Open-fronted	5x5cm (2x2in) minimum	Buildings, patios, and log and stone piles	1m (3⅓ft) and above
Robin	Open-fronted	6.5cm (2½in) minimum	Dense cover; fences, trellis, walls etc.	1.5m (5ft) and above
Starling	Medium-hole	4.5cm (1¾in) or triangular wedge	Trees and buildings	Gutter height, adjacent to roof overhang
Swift	Small-hole	Approx. 3cm (1¼in)	Buildings	Gutter height, adjacent to roof overhang
Tree sparrow	Small-hole	2.8cm (1¹⁄₁₀in)	Trees, close together in groups	2m (6½ft) and above
Wren	Open-fronted, small-hole	2.8cm (1¹⁄₁₀in) upwards	Dense cover; fences, trellis, walls etc.	1.5m (5ft) and above

INDEX

AUTHOR ACKNOWLEDGMENTS

There are many people who have supported and helped us along our journey to where we are today, too many to mention here unfortunately. But we would like to thank all of those who believe in what we do and particularly those of you who have had the faith to turn your garden into a wildlife garden. On behalf of wildlife, we thank you.

Thanks to Mum and Dad – for encouraging us into a life of horticulture and wildlife and for supporting us along the way; we wouldn't be doing what we do if it wasn't for you.

We would also like to thank those who have influenced and taught us through the years – Chris Baines for inspiring us to do the work we do, Bob Sheppard for introducing us to the magic of garden birds, Chris Howes for opening our eyes to the amazing world of Lepidoptera, Willie McLaughlin for giving us close encounters with birds in our local woods, Peter Harden for encouraging our enthusiasm for wildlife and being the best primary school teacher we could have asked for, and, finally, Stephanie at DK who discovered and encouraged us to write this book – and, of course, the rest of the team for their unwavering support.

PUBLISHER ACKNOWLEDGMENTS

DK would like to thank Vanessa Bird for indexing.

PICTURE CREDITS

The publisher would like to thank the following for their kind permission to reproduce their photographs:

page 27 Dreamstime.com: Dave Jones/Lina Sipelyte; **page 173 B** Hugh Clark/Bat Conservation Trust (www.bats.org.uk)

All other photographs © Joel and Jim Ashton, Nikki Stratton

SOURCES

page 9 European Commission (2016). "European Red List of Habitats: Terrestrial and Freshwater Habitats", page 7. https://ec.europa.eu/environment/nature/knowledge/pdf/terrestrial_EU_red_list_report.pdf

People's Trust for Endangered Species (2014). "Hedgerows: a guide to wildlife and management", page 1. https://ptes.org/wp-content/uploads/2014/06/Hedgerow-guide-web-version.pdf

RSPB (2013). "State of Nature", page 14. http://www.rspb.org.uk/Images/stateofnature_tcm9-345839.pdf

page 80 UN Environment Programme (2019). "Peatlands store twice as much carbon as all the world's forests". https://www.unenvironment.org/news-and-stories/story/peatlands-store-twice-much-carbon-all-worlds-forests

page 114 RSPB (2013), ibid.

page 115 BBC (2015). "Why meadows are worth saving". http://www.bbc.co.uk/earth/story/20150702-why-meadows-are-worth-saving

DK UK

Project editor Amy Slack
Editors Nikki Sims, Dawn Titmus
Designers Mandy Earey, Hannah Moore
Editorial assistant Millie Andrew
Illustrator Nicola Powlinwg
Senior jacket designer Nicola Powling
Jackets co-ordinator Lucy Philpott
Producer, pre-production David Almond
Senior producer Stephanie McConnell
Managing editors Stephanie Farrow, Ruth O'Rourke
Managing art editor Christine Keilty
Art director Maxine Pedliham
Publisher Mary-Clare Jerram

This edition published in 2020
First published in Great Britain in 2020 by
Dorling Kindersley Limited
DK, One Embassy Gardens, 8 Viaduct Gardens,
London, SW11 7BW

The authorised representative in the EEA is
Dorling Kindersley Verlag GmbH. Arnulfstr. 124,
80636 Munich, Germany

Copyright © 2020 Dorling Kindersley Limited
Text copyright © 2020 Jim and Joel Ashton
A Penguin Random House Company
10 9 8 7 6
007–318360–Apr/2020

A CIP catalogue record for this book
is available from the British Library.
ISBN: 978-0-2414-3581-6

Printed and bound in China

www.dk.com

ABOUT THE AUTHOR

From an early age, Joel Ashton has been immersed in the natural world. Whether he was peering into his beloved wildlife pond (which he helped dig with his mum and dad), or out exploring the local woods for wildlife on his bike, his encounters with nature taught him all about the habitats of the many animals he encountered.

Since starting Hazelwood Landscapes Ltd in 2005, Joel has devoted his working life to helping wildlife, and now has many years of experience in creating gardens and habitats for wildlife across the UK. Through observing the many specific habitats that different organisms need in order to live and thrive, Joel has gained a wealth of knowledge that enables him to turn each and every garden he designs into mini-oases of nature – even in urban areas.

Alongside the beautiful gardens he creates, Joel also gives talks and runs workshops on gardening for wildlife. Joel has featured on BBC's *Gardeners' World* and *Springwatch*, and Channel 5's *Wild Animal Rescue*, and has contributed interviews and articles to various publications including *The Telegraph*, *Country Life*, the RHS's *The Garden*, the RSPB's *Nature's Home*, and *BBC Wildlife*.

Joel is intent on inspiring as many people as possible to do their own bit for wildlife in their own outdoor space – be it a balcony, a courtyard, or several acres of land.

Whatever the job, Joel stands by the slogan: *"Working with nature, for nature"*.

FIND JOEL ASHTON ONLINE:

Websites:
hazelwoodlandscapes.com,
joelashton.com
Twitter:
@Butterfly_bros, @_joelashton
YouTube:
Wild Your Garden with Joel Ashton